"Larry Helyer's accessible book accomplishes two important tasks. First he shows why Jeremiah, of all the biblical prophets, cannot be safely disregarded by those who want faith connected to lived reality in our society. Second, he provides an introduction to the rich resources of the book of Jeremiah and shows us in compelling ways how to engage Jeremiah and link his stunning words to our own societal crisis. Helyer takes up some of the most important themes and texts of Jeremiah and does so with an alert eye concerning connections to the ministry of Jesus."

—WALTER BRUEGGEMANN
Columbia Theological Seminary

"The prophetic voice isn't supposed to be comfortable. In this imminent and clear analysis of the message of Jeremiah, Larry Helyer deftly walks the fine homiletical line between specific context and eternal truth. By doing so, he helps us see more clearly ways that we can engage the trends and tendencies of our world with the claims of the Word of God."

—PAUL H. WRIGHT
President, Jerusalem University College

"In a very readable book Helyer discusses Jeremiah the prophet by focusing on: 1) the profile of a prophet; 2) the celebrated 'temple oracles' of 609; 3) Jeremiah's symbolic actions; 4) Jeremiah and the false prophets; 5) Jeremiah's personal laments; and 6) Jeremiah's vision for the future. The prophet's hard message of judgment is laid out in all its complexities; nevertheless, a strong message of hope is discerned for the future, yet with the caution that Christians ought not 'get on the bandwagon to advocate for a third temple.' There is no temple or need for one in the New Jerusalem (Rev 21:22). Jeremiah's message finds numerous parallels in the New Testament, Church History, preaching of New England Puritanism, and other sources. Though a small book, this is one eminently worthy of critical reflection."

—JACK R. LUNDBOM

author of *Deuteronomy: Law and Covenant* (Cascade, 2017)

"Dr. Helyer presents Jeremiah as a book highly relevant and timely for the modern context. His approach, primarily topical, focuses on key themes of the book. His presentation is supported by solid biblical scholarship, well researched supplemental material, and coupled with a balanced presentation of supporting Old and New Testament texts. I especially appreciated the emphasis of Chapter Four, which deals with the tests used to determine true prophets from false ones."

—EUGENE HABECKER

President Emeritus, Taylor University

The Life and Witness of Jeremiah

The Life and Witness of Jeremiah

A Prophet for Today

LARRY R. HELYER

CASCADE Books • Eugene, Oregon

THE LIFE AND WITNESS OF JEREMIAH
A Prophet for Today

Copyright © 2019 Larry R. Helyer. All rights reserved. Except for brief quotations in critical publications or reviews, no part of this book may be reproduced in any manner without prior written permission from the publisher. Write: Permissions, Wipf and Stock Publishers, 199 W. 8th Ave., Suite 3, Eugene, OR 97401.

Cascade Books
An Imprint of Wipf and Stock Publishers
199 W. 8th Ave., Suite 3
Eugene, OR 97401

www.wipfandstock.com

PAPERBACK ISBN: 978-1-5326-1693-8
HARDCOVER ISBN: 978-1-4982-4099-4
EBOOK ISBN: 978-1-4982-4098-7

Cataloguing-in-Publication data:

Names: Helyer, Larry R., author.

Title: The life and witness of Jeremiah : a prophet for today / Larry R. Helyer.

Description: Eugene, OR : Cascade Books, 2019 | Includes bibliographical references and index.

Identifiers: ISBN 978-1-5326-1693-8 (paperback) | ISBN 978-1-4982-4099-4 (hardcover) | ISBN 978-1-4982-4098-7 (ebook)

Subjects: LCSH: Jeremiah—(Biblical prophet). | Bible.—Jeremiah.

Classification: BS1525.3 .H43 2019 (paperback) | BS1525.53 .H43 (ebook)

Manufactured in the U.S.A.   10/22/19

Scripture taken from the HOLY BIBLE, TODAY'S NEW INTERNATIONAL VERSION®. TNIV®. Copyright © 2001, 2005 by International Bible Society. Used by permission of Zondervan. All rights reserved worldwide.

Scripture quotations marked NRSV are from New Revised Standard Version Bible, copyright © 1989 National Council of the Churches of Christ in the United States of America. Used by permission. All rights reserved worldwide.

To the brothers and sisters in Christ
at Lawton Evangelical Church
Lawton, Michigan

And in memory of Avaline Kleist

Prophetic ministry has to do not primarily with addressing specific public crises but with addressing, in season and out of season, the dominant crisis that is enduring and resilient, of having our alternative vocation co-opted and domesticated.
—Walter Brueggemann, *The Prophetic Imagination*

It seems wrong—almost sinful—to ask anyone to enjoy Jeremiah. Through much of the book you will be weeping with him, and seldom will you be able to laugh with him. But by the time you finish, you will have experienced a strange kind of enjoyment through getting to know a very human prophet.
—William J. Petersen, *Jeremiah: The Prophet Who Wouldn't Quit*

Contents

Preface | ix
Acknowledgments | xiii
List of Abbreviations | xv

1 Profile of a Prophet | 1
2 The Temple Sermon | 19
3 Jeremiah's Symbolic Actions | 39
4 Jeremiah and the False Prophets | 58
5 Jeremiah's Complaints | 76
6 Jeremiah's Vision of the Future | 99
7 Epilogue | 124

Appendix | 127
Bibliography | 131
Index | 135

Preface

For nearly thirty years I taught a course on Hebrew prophets to undergrads at Taylor University. The prophet I most enjoyed introducing to students was Jeremiah. I made a mental note that someday I wanted to write a short book on his life and message. This book is my attempt to introduce Jeremiah to a larger audience.

So, what is it about Jeremiah that commends him to a modern readership? For one thing, he was a superb communicator, although I readily admit, contemporary readers are not likely to immediately latch on to Jeremiah as their literary muse. His writing style diverges considerably from that of best-selling poets and novelists. But more than that, Jeremiah is just plain difficult to read.[1] As it turns out, it's the second longest book in the Bible (after Psalms), but that isn't the main problem; the difficulty lies in the nature of the book itself, an anthology of sermons and disconnected narratives about his life.

Sermons, to be effective, must speak into the time and place in which they are delivered. Accordingly, they are very much culturally conditioned pieces of writing, and most readers lack the requisite historical and social background with which to make sense of this sixth-century BC preacher. For the same reason, the sermons of Cotton Mather, one of the pulpit giants of the Founding Fathers era of American history, rarely connect with readers

---

[1]. "It has often been called one of the most unreadable books in the Bible" (Smith, "Book of Jeremiah," 1). Smith gives a good overview of the difficulties one faces when reading the book of Jeremiah and offers some helpful guidance on making sense of the book as a whole.

Preface

today. As in Mather, so in Jeremiah, the figures of speech, metaphors, allusions and historical references blow right by without full comprehension. Compounding the problem, Jeremiah's sermons and the narratives about him lack chronological order. Sermons preached near the end of Jeremiah's ministry occur in the early part of the book, and sermons preached early on are placed in later chapters. The same is true with regard to the prose narratives; the reader is toggled back and forth between different time periods. Without a study Bible or commentary, following the flow of Jeremiah's thought or the course of his ministry is well-nigh impossible. I hope my introduction assists the reader to make sense of Jeremiah's message—the required effort is well worth it.

First of all, the poetry of Jeremiah is exquisite and possesses a timeless quality.[2] In spite of the chronological and cultural distance, if one perseveres, Jeremiah starts to get under your skin. The gap between then and now closes, and readers begin to hear his heart. For those who discover this sweet spot, Jeremiah becomes a favorite fellow traveler. This book is written for those who search and find (Matt 7:8).

Second, Jeremiah is truly one of the all-time heroes of the faith. Though not mentioned by name in the famous hall of faith chapter in Hebrews 11, he certainly was known to the writer of Hebrews and included in the anonymous category of "the prophets" who "faced jeers and flogging, and even chains and imprisonment" (Heb 11:36). Few have had to tread as difficult a path as Jeremiah in the performance of his calling to be a spokesperson of the Lord.[3] His courage and perseverance were remarkable, and he rightly belongs in that select group who comprise "a great cloud of witnesses" (Heb 12:1).

Third, Jeremiah was an astute religious and social critic of his time. What is so striking about his writing is its contemporary

---

2. Brueggemann calls him "this most eloquent of all prophets" (*Prophetic Imagination*, 51).

3. "No other prophet of Judah or Israel was placed in Jeremiah's position. He stands alone in circumstances of the most desperate and heart-breaking nature faithfully and unflinchingly declaring the word of Jehovah . . ." (*New Analytical Bible*, 357).

Preface

relevance in spite of its cultural distance. Perhaps this more than any other feature commends him to modern readers. What goes around comes around, and the ills that beset his small nation plague our own in epidemic proportions. When viewed through the lens of the prophet Jeremiah, our current political crisis in the United States assumes an even more ominous threat. Jeremiah's urgent appeal, however, if sincerely acted upon, offers an antidote to the ethical, moral, and spiritual malaise so endemic in our culture.

This introduction to Jeremiah is not a commentary; it's a pastoral exposition of selected themes, a portal into the world and rhetoric of Jeremiah. I've tried to keep it relatively short. Commentaries on Jeremiah tend to run into the hundreds of pages. Few readers attempt, much less finish, these learned and lengthy works—they wind up on the shelves of libraries and specialists in biblical studies. I don't disparage such works; indeed, I feel obligated to inform the reader that I've tried to do my homework and have learned much from interacting with scholarly literature devoted to Jeremiah. But my primary audience is not the specialist, it's the lay reader who wants to gain a better understanding of what made this prophet tick—and what ticked him off! In light of that, I've tried to avoid scholarly jargon and extended discussion of technical matters lest they interfere with grasping the essential message of this literary and theological giant. Footnotes have been kept to a minimum. Above all, I hope the reader hears the heart of this choice servant of Yahweh and responds to his enduring message. To that end, generous use of quotations from Jeremiah are incorporated. "Whoever has ears, let them hear" (Matt 11:15; 13:9, 43).

I wrote this book in my study under the disconsolate gaze of Jeremiah. Literally. Hanging above my desk is a reproduction of Rembrandt's famous painting *Jeremiah Lamenting the Destruction of Jerusalem* (1630). Rembrandt's Jeremiah doesn't actually look at the viewer. He rests his weary head on his left hand and stares blankly at his feet. His left elbow rests on a bound copy of a book titled *Bibel* (German for Bible), reminding us of that transcendent reality that transformed Jeremiah's life: "The word of the Lord came

Preface

to me." In the foreground is a golden bowl with chalices and cups, probably representing temple vessels. Rembrandt depicts Jeremiah sitting in a cave with its opening to his right, the viewer's left.[4] Through this opening, one discerns in the dark background flames rising from Jerusalem and a domed building, almost certainly the temple. Barely discernible, a man with his fists clenched over his eyes stands outside the walls. This is probably the last Judean king, Zedekiah, whose eyes were gouged out after witnessing the execution of his sons (Jer 52:9–11). Three figures, with robes and miters, stand at the mouth of a cave beneath the doomed building. They probably represent priests hiding the ark of the covenant beneath the temple, a tradition widely circulated in the Jewish community and no doubt known to Rembrandt. The painting is executed in dark, somber tones, so typical of Rembrandt, capturing with his masterful touch a moment of heartbreaking sadness.

The reproduction was given to me by a Christian friend, Avaline Kleist. She was going through a difficult time of deep depression, and the painting seemed to accentuate her despair. She asked me if I would take it. I was happy to accept. I positioned it above my desk. Sometime later—I'm not sure if there was a conscious connection—I decided to write this book on Jeremiah. I wish Rembrandt had painted another rendition of Jeremiah, one depicting him awakening from his dream about the restoration of Israel (Jer 31:26). I try to imagine how Rembrandt might have captured that moment of deep pleasure on Jeremiah's face. A number of years after Avaline gave me the painting, she went to "be with Christ, which is better by far" (Phil 1:23). I have no doubt that after awakening from her coma, and finding herself in the presence of the Lord, she too experienced deep pleasure. This book is dedicated to her memory.

---

4. There is a cave in Jerusalem, across the street and not far from the Damascus Gate of the Old City, traditionally called "Jeremiah's Grotto." Rembrandt was no doubt aware of this tradition brought back to Holland by Christian pilgrims.

Acknowledgments

I am indebted to my students who have studied the Hebrew prophets with me over the years (1979–2008). Their engagement with the text and perceptive questions added more than they will ever know to the satisfaction of teaching. Most of those classes were in classrooms at Taylor University in Upland, Indiana. One semester, however, I had the privilege of teaching a course on the Hebrew prophets at Jerusalem University College in Jerusalem, Israel. Dr. Paul Wright, the president of JUC, invited me to be an adjunct professor in the fall semester of 2010. He personally led the students taking Historical and Geographical Settings on field trips as part of the course requirements and graciously invited me to accompany the students, even allowing opportunities to share insights from the prophets where relevant. He also assisted me in leading field trips in conjunction with my course. There is nothing like being able to teach the Bible on location. Many thanks, Paul, for the invitation, encouragement, and friendship over the years. May you and Diane enjoy a rich and rewarding retirement!

As always, my best encourager and sharp-eyed proofreader is my beloved wife, Joyce. She and I share a passionate love for the Holy Land and its people. We continue to enjoy leading Christian pilgrims on tours in this amazing land. Thank you, dear wife and companion of fifty-four years, for all you do!

Special thanks to the excellent team at Cascade Books. Having studied for a year at the University of Oregon (go Ducks!), and having a sister who still lives in Eugene, I often see in my mind's eye

Acknowledgments

the wonderful setting in which you folks go about your daily tasks of publishing. After the Holy Land, the Northwest must surely be God's special country. Thanks, editorial staff, for your expertise in seeing this manuscript through to the printed page.

List of Abbreviations

BIBLICAL TEXTS AND VERSIONS

GNB	Good News Bible
KJV	King James Version
1 Macc	1 Maccabees
2 Macc	2 Maccabees
MT	Masoretic Text of the Hebrew Bible/Old Testament
NET	New English Translation
NRSV	New Revised Standard Version
NT	New Testament
OT	Old Testament
TNIV	Today's New International Version

OTHER ANCIENT TEXTS

Adv. Haer.	Irenaeus, *Adversus haereses* (*Against Heresies*)
ANET	*Ancient Near Eastern Texts Relating to the Old Testament*. Edited by James B. Pritchard. 3rd ed., with suppl. Princeton: Princeton University Press, 1969.
b.	Babylonian Talmud

LIST OF ABBREVIATIONS

COS	*The Context of Scripture.* Edited by William Hallo and Lawson Younger. 3 vols. Leiden: Brill, 1997–2002.
Hist. eccl.	Eusebius, *Ecclesiastical History*
m.	Mishnah
S. 'Olam Rab.	*Seder 'Olam Rabbah*
Tg.	Targum
Šeqal.	*Šeqalim* (Shekels)
y.	Jerusalem Talmud

SECONDARY SOURCES

AB	The Anchor Bible
BAR	*Biblical Archaeology Review*
EBC	Expositor's Bible Commentary
IDB	*The Interpreter's Dictionary of the Bible.* Edited by G. A. Buttrick. 4 vols. Nashville: Abingdon, 1962.
IEJ	*Israel Exploration Journal*
JETS	*Journal of the Evangelical Theological Society*
NEAEHL	*The New Encyclopedia of Archaeological Excavations in the Holy Land.* Edited by Ephraim Stern. 4 vols. Jerusalem: Carta, 1993.
NIVAC	New International Version Application Commentary
VT	*Vetus Testamentum*
WTJ	*Westminster Theological Journal*

1

Profile of a Prophet

BIRTH AND BACKGROUND

In about 640 BC, a priest named Hilkiah rejoiced at the birth of a son. Perhaps while performing his priestly duties at the Jerusalem temple, he received the glad news: "A child is born to you—a son!" (Jer 20:15).[1] How ironic that his new son, Jeremiah, would one day stand in the sacred precincts of the Jerusalem temple and announce its utter destruction (Jer 7:14).[2]

Even the meaning of Jeremiah's name evokes irony. *Yirmĕyāhû* probably means something like "Yahweh will hurl or cast."[3] Imag-

---

1. The priests were organized into twenty-four divisions and served a seven-day stint biannually (1 Chr 9:25; 24:1–19). In addition, during the three annual pilgrimage festivals of Passover, Weeks, and Tabernacles (Deut 16), probably all the priests were on hand to serve the large number of worshipers.

2. Most scholars think it unlikely this Hilkiah was also the high priest in the days of King Josiah (2 Kgs 22:4), but if they are one and the same the irony is even sharper.

3. The ending of Jeremiah's name in Hebrew, *yāhû*, is a shortened form of the Tetragrammaton, the four Hebrew consonants of God's personal name (*yhwh*). Scholars are generally agreed that the sacred name should be vocalized in English as "Yahweh." English versions of the Bible, however, usually render

ine you are in a bowling alley, watching a bowler get a strike—all the pins are knocked over and go flying. That, in one "striking" word picture, captures the impact of Jeremiah's preaching!

The irony runs even deeper. During the settlement of the land of Canaan, Anathoth, Jeremiah's birthplace, was designated a priestly town (Josh 2:18).[4] One of Anathoth's most celebrated citizens was the priest Abiathar, who served with distinction throughout the storied career of David. Two of David's mighty warriors were also from Anathoth (2 Sam 23:27; 1 Chr 11:28). Unfortunately, Abiathar's priestly service ended in disgrace when he supported Adonijah as David's successor. Solomon, who prevailed in the power struggle for succession, banished Abiathar to his hometown for treason (1 Kgs 2:26–27). Abiathar traced his ancestry back to the hapless high priest Eli in the days of Samuel (1 Sam 1–4). An unnamed prophet appeared at the sanctuary of Shiloh and pronounced the destruction of the family of Eli because he tolerated the immoral and irreligious behavior of his sons, Hophni and Phinehas (1 Sam 2:30–33). The prophecy was fulfilled when Saul massacred the priests living at Nob. Only Abiathar escaped with his life, in accordance with the prophetic word (1 Sam 2:33). With uncanny similarity, Jeremiah was also spared the sword but suffered royal disfavor and banishment as a traitor. In short, a troubled family history precedes the career of Jeremiah and reappears during his turbulent ministry. In fact, his relationship with most of the Jerusalem priesthood was fraught with bitter antagonism and opposition.

---

it as "Lord" in small caps. In my book, I will use "Yahweh," except when quoting from the English text of the NT, where the word "Lord" is used. The name Yahweh conveys the idea of the self-existent one and is interpreted to Moses as meaning "I Am Who I Am" (Exod 3:14). Many Hebrew names in the Bible, esp. of Judahites, are theophoric (lit. "bearing the name of God").

4. Anathoth is either the modern Arab town of *Anata* or *Ras el-Kharrubeh*, a site less than half a mile away.

PROFILE OF A PROPHET

CALL AND COMMISSION

We know nothing of Jeremiah's early childhood. When he was about twelve or thirteen years of age, Jeremiah's world was turned upside down. Yahweh summoned Jeremiah to be his spokesperson, "a prophet to the nations" (Jer 1:5). The time of Jeremiah's call may be cinched down fairly securely. The thirteenth year of Josiah's reign was either 627 or 626 BC (cf. Jer 25:3). About the same time, Ashurbanipal king of Assyria died, ushering in a steady decline in Assyrian hegemony over the Near East (Assyria was located more or less in modern Iraq). In this power vacuum two powerful states vied for supremacy, Egypt and Babylon (southern Iraq and Kuwait). Babylon would ultimately prevail, and tiny Judah, like a pinball, battered and buffeted between these two super powers. Jeremiah's preaching unfolds in the political and historical context of this power struggle, and his stance on how Judah should position herself in the ensuing conflict elicited visceral enmity and opposition from Judah's political and religious leadership; in fact, a majority of Jerusalem's citizens deemed Jeremiah public enemy number one.

Jeremiah's call, narrated in first person, falls into several distinct parts:

Yahweh's Preordination

A standard formula, validating the messenger as a genuine prophet, introduces the call narrative: "The word of the LORD came to me, saying" (Jer 1:4).[5] Jeremiah's testimony makes clear that he neither sought nor anticipated such a summons. What he now recognizes in hindsight is that long before his birth, Yahweh had destined him to assume the prophet's mantle. In this Jeremiah is not alone. Running throughout OT Scripture is an underlying truth—God has a plan and purpose that he realizes through predestined people. God chose the patriarchs and matriarchs, the

---

5. See also Isa 6:8-9; Ezek 2:1—3:27; Hos 1:1; Joel 1:1; Jonah 1:1; Mic 1:1; Zeph 1:1; Hag 1:1; Zech 1:1; Mal 1:1.

judges and early kings, the Aaronic priesthood and the prophets. In no case did these elect individuals or families determine their own destiny by deeds or desires. The NT underscores the same truth (cf. Rom 9:8–18); in fact, we find a very close parallel in the Apostle Paul's testimony concerning his call to be an apostle: "But when God, who had set me apart before I was born and called me through his grace, was pleased to reveal his Son to me, so that I might proclaim him among the Gentiles . . ." (Gal 1:15–16 NRSV). I think Paul consciously composed his call and commission with Jeremiah in mind. Three items in particular draw attention to the striking similarity: a prenatal call, a personal divine revelation, and a preaching mission to the Gentiles (nations). If we bring in Dr. Luke's account of Paul's conversion in the book of Acts, a fourth distinctive element common to both becomes apparent: they were destined to suffer persecution in the performance of their mission.[6]

Jeremiah's Protest

Jeremiah, like others called into Yahweh's service, feels totally inadequate for the task. One recalls the reluctance of Moses and Isaiah to serve as Yahweh's spokesperson.[7] Jeremiah's objection centers on his youthful inexperience: "Truly I do not know how to speak, for I am only a boy" (Jer 1:6 NRSV). I've earlier mentioned that Jeremiah was probably about twelve or thirteen years old when he was called. This is based on the Hebrew word *na'ar* that Jeremiah uses to identify himself—the same word used in the account of Samuel's call: "The boy [*na'ar*] Samuel ministered before the LORD . . ." (1 Sam 3:1). In all likelihood, then, both Samuel and Jeremiah were not yet adults when summoned into service.[8] In later Jewish tradition, of course, the thirteenth year is when a Jewish male is reckoned as fully responsible for his actions and becomes a full-fledged member of the covenant community, a bar mitzvah

---

6. Jer 1:8, 17–19; Acts 9:16; 26:17.

7. See Exod 4:10–17; Isa 6:5.

8. So also Lundbom, *Prophet Like Moses*, 2.

("son of commandment"). What is interesting is that when Jesus was twelve years old, he showed up "in the temple courts, sitting among the teachers, listening to them and asking them questions. Everyone who heard him was amazed at his understanding and his answers" (Luke 2:46–47).[9] Like Jeremiah before him, during his ministry Jesus harshly condemned the Jerusalem temple and religious leaders and predicted the destruction of the temple itself.[10] We will have occasion to draw a number of parallels between Jeremiah and Jesus as we proceed in this study.

Yahweh's Provision

Yahweh brushes aside Jeremiah's protestation and commissions him for the task.[11] The divine imperative is unmistakable and non-negotiable: "You must go . . . and say whatever I command you" (Jer 1:7). As always, when Yahweh summons, he also strengthens those summoned. One thinks of Joshua, who, after the death of Moses, was entrusted with the daunting task of leading an invasion of the land of Canaan. Joshua's fear of failure was met with this ringing word of assurance: "No one shall be able to stand against you all the days of your life. As I was with Moses, so I will be with you: I will not fail you or forsake you. Be strong and courageous; for you shall put this people in possession of the land that I swore to their ancestors to give them" (Josh 1:5–6). In like manner, Jeremiah receives this word of assurance: "Do not be afraid of them, for I am with you to deliver you, says the LORD" (Jer 1:8), and "'They will fight against you but will not overcome you, for I am with you and will rescue you,' declares the LORD" (Jer 1:19).

9. It is worth noting that on average most people become Christians at the age of thirteen. See "When Americans Become Christians," which presents the results of a poll conducted by the National Association of Evangelicals (Spring 2015): http://nae.net/when-americans-become-christians.

10. Matt 21:12–27; 24:1–3; Mark 11:15–19; 13:1–2; Luke 19:45–46; 21:5–7; John 2:13–17.

11. "God does not send us into the dangerous and exacting life of faith because we are qualified; he chooses us in order to qualify us for what he wants us to be and do." Peterson, *Run with the Horses*, 51.

Yahweh's Proclamation

So what is the basic message Yahweh wants Jeremiah to preach? Six verbs form the core of Jeremiah's proclamation, concisely summarizing the content of all the recorded messages in the book. The six verbs are in the form of three couplets, the first two being negative and the last positive. They are: uproot and tear down, destroy and overthrow, build and plant. Not surprisingly, a majority of Jeremiah's sermons are judgment oracles. In these oracles the nation as a whole comes under scathing criticism. Top-down or bottom-up makes no difference; leaders and people alike fall under condemnation (Jer 5:1–5), though clearly the political and religious leadership bear the primary responsibility for the deplorable moral decadence and receive the brunt of Jeremiah's arraignment.[12] As we will see, Jeremiah, like the other writing prophets, rings the changes with remarkable variety and rhetorical effectiveness.[13] Jeremiah's rhetoric merits the highest marks and invites repeated reading to appreciate his literary skill. Thankfully, Jeremiah also receives and delivers words of comfort and consolation for the repentant remnant. In the end, Yahweh will build and plant and, consistent with his covenant faithfulness, establish a new covenant with his renewed people (Jer 30–31).

Yahweh's Program

How will Yahweh bring about his proclamation of judgment? Jeremiah's call is accompanied by two visionary experiences. In prophetic call narratives, visions play a prominent role.[14]

---

12. See Jer 3:15; 10:21; 12:10; 23:1; 50:6.

13. Readers may not be familiar with the expression "ring the changes." It refers to ringing a set of bells in a church belfry according to various patterns and sequences. English parish churches in the Anglican tradition are well-known for this practice.

14. Moses saw a burning bush (Exod 3:1–6); Amos saw a locust plague, fire, and a plumb line (Amos 7:1–9); Isaiah saw Yahweh in his heavenly throne room (Isa 6:1–13); Joel saw an approaching swarm of locusts (Joel 1:1—2:11); and Ezekiel saw the heavenly throne chariot (Ezek 1:4–28).

PROFILE OF A PROPHET

Jeremiah's first vision suggests the approximate time of year he was called. Yahweh asks, "What do you see, Jeremiah?" His response: "the branch of an almond tree" (Jer 1:11). Most likely, the almond tree was singled out when its distinctive white blossoms first appear, usually in late January or early February. I've visited Israel during this particular time of year and can attest to their welcome appearance as harbingers of the verdant spring soon to come in the Holy Land. In Jeremiah's vision, however, the almond blossoms serve not as signs of spring but as sinister sentinels: Yahweh is about to visit the land in judgment and retribution. In fact, the point of the vision is not the timing of Jeremiah's call at all; it's the word for the almond tree itself, namely, *shaqed*. Employing a pun, Yahweh says, "I am watching over my word to perform it" (NRSV). The verbal idea of "watching over" is conveyed by the word *shoqed*. The similarity in sound between *shaqed* and *shoqed* resonates for a native speaker of Hebrew. The point being underscored is the certainty of fulfillment. What Yahweh proclaims by his word will most assuredly come to pass.

And what is it that shall surely come to pass? The second vision, a pot of scalding hot water spilling over the land of Judah, vividly portends an invasion of Judah from the north. This was the usual attack route of neighboring states lying to the north and east of the land of Israel.[15] The aggressive and militaristic empire of Assyria, the scourge of the northern kingdom of Israel—and, for nearly a century, the overlord of her vassal state Judah—had invaded Israel from the north. But during Jeremiah's ministry, Assyria was in decline. A new superpower was emerging: the Neo-Babylonian Empire, centered in the ancient land of Sumer, was now rapidly encroaching on the lands formerly subjugated by the Assyrian rod of Yahweh's anger (cf. Isa 10:5). In fact, Josiah

---

15. One thinks of Chedorlaomer's coalition in the days of Abram (Gen 14); King Cushan-Rishathaim of Aram-naharaim (modern Syria) in the days of the Judges (Judg 3:7–11); King Ben-hadad of Aram (present-day Syria; see 1 Kgs 15:20); another Ben-hadad of Aram with a coalition of kings (2 Kgs 20:1, 26); Hazael of Aram (2 Kgs 10:32–33); King Pul (Tiglath-Pileser III) of Assyria (present-day Iraq; see 2 Kgs 15:19, 29); King Shalmanezer of Assyria (2 Kgs 17:3–6; 18:9–12); and finally, King Sennacherib of Assyria (2 Kgs 18:13).

threw off the Assyrian yoke and declared Judah's independence. He might even have harbored hopes of restoring the old Davidic boundaries of a united Israel. These hopes were, of course, short-lived, dashed in the ensuing power struggle between Egypt and Babylon, during which Pharaoh Neco II snuffed out Josiah's life at Megiddo (2 Kgs 23:29–30). Although Jeremiah doesn't initially name the aggressor, he later announces that Babylon, under the charismatic and dynamic Nebuchadnezzar, will be the power that overflows and scalds the land of Judah (Jer 20:4; 25:8–9).

Jerusalem and the leading cities of Judah are destined to undergo devastating sieges resulting in death by sword, famine, and pestilence, and deportation of the fortunate few who survive. Divine justification for such desolation centers in a fundamental failure of the Judeans: "their wickedness in forsaking me, in burning incense to other gods and in worshiping what their hands have made" (Jer 1:16). In short, the ultimate sanction for failure to keep the stipulations of the Sinai covenant is executed by Yahweh, Israel's sovereign overlord. He expels them from his land with just cause; they have abandoned him, the only true and living God.[16]

HIGHLIGHTS OF JEREMIAH'S MINISTRY

Jeremiah's forty-year ministry began in the hopeful days of the young reformer king Josiah and lasted beyond the tragic times of the vacillating king Zedekiah. The superscription mentions the three kings of Judah who mark significant phases of Jeremiah's ministry. These warrant further comment.[17]

---

16. On the sanctions for noncompliance with the Sinai stipulations, see Lev 26:1–39, esp. vv. 31–33; Deut 28:15–68. For background on the Sinai covenant as a suzerainty treaty between Yahweh and Israel, see Helyer, *Yesterday*, 149–60.

17. Omitted from the list are Jehoahaz (609–608 BC) and Jehoiachin (597 BC). Jehoahaz, son and successor to Josiah, reigned only three months before Pharaoh Neco deposed and deported him to Egypt, where he remained in captivity until his death. Jeremiah composed a brief lament over his fate (Jeremiah calls him Shallum, probably his personal name), accompanied by a divine oracle confirming its certainty (Jer 22:10–12). Jehoiachin fared no

PROFILE OF A PROPHET

Josiah

Surprisingly, few of Jeremiah's recorded messages are dated to the time of Josiah (640–609 BC). Given the accolades bestowed upon Josiah (2 Kgs 23:25), Jeremiah's personal esteem for the king (Jer 22:15–16), and the laments he composed to commemorate Josiah's tragic death (2 Chr 35:25), one may well wonder why Jeremiah "takes so little notice of him."[18] MacLean suggests that "Jeremiah looked beneath the surface and saw that Josiah's real goal was the establishment of a political kingdom."[19] In my view, there is much more to it than that. Jeremiah wholeheartedly supported Josiah's reform movement, but disillusionment slowly dimmed optimism. In reality, things weren't going well at all. The young prophet became increasingly troubled by the superficial nature of the reform (Jer 3:1–10).[20] Although Josiah himself is not singled out for criticism, the nation is indicted for failing to repent and conform to the stipulations of the Sinai covenant. Jeremiah is sickened by their hypocrisy and in no uncertain terms reminds them that such two-faced behavior will not be tolerated by the great sovereign of Sinai. A day of reckoning is in the offing (Jer 4:3–4, 6–7).

It's during the post-Josiah years that Jeremiah almost single-handedly emerges to confront the nation's apostasy and is catapulted into the public limelight.[21] The messages delivered during

---

better; he too reigned only three months before being carried off into captivity in Babylon, where he remained until he died. Jeremiah refers to him as King Coniah and announces his exile and the fact that none of his descendants would ever sit on the throne of David again (Jer 22:24–30; cf. 24:1 where he is called King Jeconiah).

18. MacLean, "Josiah," 2:999.

19. MacLean, "Josiah," 2:999.

20. "It didn't take Jeremiah long to realize that the reform was only skin-deep. Everything had changed, but nothing had changed. The outward changes had been enormous; the inward changes were imperceptible." Peterson, *Run with the Horses*, 64.

21. In Josiah's eighteenth year (622 BC), after hearing the contents of the Book of the Law and being greatly alarmed, he requested that inquiry be made about the consequences of national apostasy. Interestingly, the religious and political leaders inquire of Huldah the prophetess. She relays a message that

this period represent the mature Jeremiah, who must now be "a fortified city, an iron pillar and a bronze wall to stand against the whole land—against the kings of Judah, its officials, its priests and the people of the land" (Jer 1:18). This will be Jeremiah's finest hour, but also his most agonizing.

Jehoiakim

Things come to a head in the days of Jehoiakim, when prophet and king memorably lock horns. Jehoiakim obviously has no commitment to his father's reform agenda and sets a quite different course. He seeks to be inclusive in religious matters and turns his attention to realpolitik (foreign policy dictated by expediency rather than ethics and morality). In short, his goal is to be a survivor and to enjoy the good life afforded by his political office.

Jeremiah, however, acts as a burr under his saddle. A striking example appears in Jer 22:13–19. Jehoiakim envisions himself as a new Solomon and accordingly undertakes to build a grand new palace. This building project probably took place about two miles southwest of the ancient city of Jerusalem at a site called Ramat Raḥel.[22] Escaping the narrow confines of the Ophel ridge in the City of David, Jehoiakim relocates to a more spacious site with a superb view of the surrounding hill country of Judah, the Judean desert, the Jordan Valley, and the mountains of Moab. Jeremiah berates him for grandeur and greed. Diverting funds desperately

---

chimes in precisely with what Jeremiah will steadfastly proclaim to the end (2 Kgs 22:16). The only consolation lay in the fact that Josiah would not live to witness the catastrophe (22:19-20). Zephaniah, an older, contemporary prophet during the days of Josiah, strikes the same notes as Jeremiah (Zeph 3:1-2). Both Huldah and Zephaniah were Jerusalemites.

22. Iron Age II remains of a large citadel and palace complex surrounded by a massive wall have been excavated at Ramat Raḥel. See Barkay, "Ramat Raḥel," 1479–84. See also the website of the Ramat Raḥel Archaeological Project: http://www.tau.ac.il/~rmtrachl/archaeology%20of%20site.htm. Though it is still under debate, I think Aharoni is correct that Ramat Raḥel is the biblical site of Beth-Haccherem. "Excavations at Ramat Rahel," 102–11, 137–57. See Jer 6:1; Neh 3:14.

PROFILE OF A PROPHET

needed for the state, Jehoiakim spends them on personal luxury. He makes up for the shortfall by exploiting the poor and extorting the rich. His totally narcissistic behavior falls far short of the justice and righteousness performed by his father, Josiah. Jeremiah utters a divine woe and judgment oracle upon the self-centered regent in which Jehoiakim receives his just recompense: the indignity of an unlamented death and the ignominy of an anonymous burial outside the city walls of Jerusalem. So much for the pretensions of the powerful.

As you would expect, Jehoiakim did not take kindly to Jeremiah's rebukes. Nowhere is this more dramatically illustrated than in an episode narrated in chapter 36. The lead-up to this clash is set in the fateful fourth year of Jehoiakim (605 BC), a watershed in the Ancient Near East. Nebuchadnezzar decisively defeated the coalition armies of Egypt and Assyria stationed at Carchemish on the Euphrates River, and the Neo-Babylonian Empire began to assert its control over the entire region. Jehoiakim suddenly awoke to a new political reality—Babylon was threatening to become his new overlord.

Against that backdrop, the word of Yahweh comes to Jeremiah. He summons Baruch to take down dictation in a scroll.[23] Jehoiakim had previously issued a restraining order banning Jeremiah from the temple courtyards (Jer 36:5). We'll have more to say about the famous temple sermon (Jer 7, 26) and its aftermath in the next chapter. Jehoiakim calls for a national day of fasting and prayer in light of the looming crisis. Jeremiah resorts to plan B: Baruch, his trusted secretary, reads aloud his dictated message at some point during the public gathering. The effect is like a bomb going off in the temple. One of the royal officials, Micaiah, rushes off and delivers a summary of what was said to the royal officials assembled in the chamber of Elishama the secretary. They in turn dispatch a messenger to Baruch demanding that he personally

---

23. Scholars have long labored to discover the literary relationship between the scroll of Jer 36 and the final edition of Jeremiah, resulting in a wide array of conclusions. I share Brueggemann's assessment of these efforts: "I regard all such 'historical' conclusions as useless and am interested in the dramatic portrayal of the narrative itself." Brueggemann, "Texts That Linger," 186.

The Life and Witness of Jeremiah

appear and read the scroll in their presence. Alarmed and shaken by its contents, the officials quickly decide that the king must be informed immediately because so many people in the temple courtyard have already heard its explosive contents. To use mixed metaphors, the cat is out of the bag and the ball is now in the king's court.

Jehoiakim's calloused response speaks volumes about his spiritual condition. Jeremiah's scroll is retrieved from the secretary's chamber and, for the third time that day, read aloud—this time to the king himself.[24] We should note at this point that King Jehoiakim is residing in the royal palace located on the Ophel, the ridge just below the Temple Mount, and not out at his grand palace on Ramat Raḥel. Obviously, it was necessary for the king to be near the temple during this national assembly and fast. We are also informed that it was during December and the king was seated before an indoor brazier for warmth. In this setting, one of the more memorable moments of Scripture unfolds: "Whenever Jehudi had read three or four columns of the scroll, the king cut them off with a scribe's knife and threw them into the firepot, until the entire scroll was burned in the fire" (Jer 36:23). Jehoiakim's brazen disregard for the word of Yahweh stands in stark contrast to the response of his father, Josiah, when the Book of the Law was read out in his presence: "When the king [Josiah] heard the words of the Book of the Law, he tore his robes" (2 Kgs 22:11). But in

---

24. Brown says that "there is no need to assume that the events recorded in vv. 8–23 all transpire on the same day; if they did, the scroll would have been read three times in one day, whereas two readings on the first day is the most likely scenario." Brown, *Jeremiah–Ezekiel*, 483. Perhaps, but there is no need to assume that it couldn't have taken place on the same day, which is certainly the impression one gets on a face-value reading. As noted above, the king is probably not residing far from the location of the secretary's chamber, so it wouldn't take long to transfer the scroll. Furthermore, in the days of the return from exile, Ezra the scribe publicly read from the Book of the Law "from daybreak until noon" (Neh 8:3)—about six hours! In light of this, there can hardly be any objection to three readings of an early version of the book of Jeremiah in one day. Conjectures as to the length of this scroll vary from six to twenty-five chapters. Hicks estimates a scroll of some twelve to fifteen columns amounting to about eighteen to twenty-four chapters. Hicks, "*Delet* and *megillah*," 46–66.

the case of Jehoiakim, "The king and all his attendants who heard all these words showed no fear, nor did they tear their clothes" (Jer 36:24). Furthermore, Jehoiakim issues a warrant for the arrest of both Baruch and Jeremiah. Cryptically, the episode concludes with this brief comment: "But the Lord had hidden them" (Jer 36:26). Yahweh keeps his promise to Jeremiah: "'They will fight against you but will not overcome you, for I am with you and will rescue you,' declares the Lord" (Jer 1:19). As for Baruch, who was now also in great fear for his life (Jer 45:1–3), Yahweh likewise assures him of personal safety (Jer 45:5).

Zedekiah

The superscription to the book indicates that Jeremiah's ministry in Jerusalem continued until Zedekiah, the last king of Judah, and the survivors of the siege of Jerusalem were exiled to Babylon in 587/586 BC. During his reign, things go from bad to worse. Zedekiah himself seems not to have been as antagonistic toward Jeremiah as Jehoiakim. In fact, several times he consults with Jeremiah for a word from Yahweh (Jer 37:3, 17; 38:14). The problem lay in his precarious political position and lack of personal courage.[25] As Zedekiah sought to steer a survival course between Scylla and Charybdis (i.e., the pro-Egyptian and pro-Babylonian factions), Jeremiah was allowed to be swept overboard, so to speak. When Jeremiah was falsely arrested for desertion, beaten, and imprisoned in a cistern house made into a cell, the king did not intervene (37:12–16). Later, during a secret meeting, Jeremiah pleads with the king to be removed from his cell. Finally, Zedekiah acquiesces and orders Jeremiah transferred to the court of the guard and allows a daily ration of bread (Jer 37:17–21).

Unfortunately, Jeremiah's enemies prevail upon the king to turn Jeremiah over to them because, in their view, he is a traitor who undermines morale by prophesying a Babylonian victory. The cowardly king relents: "He is in your hands . . . the king can do

---

25. "The man was a marshmallow. He received impressions from anyone who pushed hard enough." Peterson, *Run with the Horses*, 161.

nothing to oppose you" (Jer 38:5). Zedekiah's abandonment leads to Jeremiah's darkest hours. Thrown into a cistern in which there was no water, only mud, he sinks into the muck. Lacking water and bread, he would have died an agonizing death had not a courageous court official, Ebed-melech the Ethiopian, come to his rescue.[26] Providentially, Ebed-melech was able to gain Zedekiah's ear and plead for Jeremiah's life (Jer 38:7-8).[27] To his credit, the king orders a secret mission to transfer Jeremiah back to the court of the guard (Jer 38:13). For his bravery, Ebed-melech receives divine assurance through Jeremiah that his life will be spared, because he trusted in Yahweh (Jer 39:17-18).

Jeremiah survived the ordeal, a brutal eighteen-month siege (Jer 38:28; cf. 2 Kgs 25:3; Lam 2:20-21). Despite the fact that he persistently prophesied the fall of Jerusalem, in the end, he had no stomach for a reproachful "I told you so." Rather, he was sick to his stomach and his heart was broken (Jer 4:19). The deeply moving laments in the book of Lamentations express his bitter anguish: "My eyes are spent with weeping; my stomach churns; my bile is poured out on the ground because of the destruction of my people..." (Lam 2:11 NRSV).

Zedekiah, however, suffered a tragic fate, just as Jeremiah had prophesied. Captured in a futile attempt to flee Jerusalem, he was conveyed to Nebuchadnezzar's headquarters and sentenced. His sons were killed before his eyes and then his eyes were put out. He was bound and led off to Babylon, bereft and blinded. In the end, he was buried in Babylon. Jeremiah and Baruch both wound up in Egypt, having been dragged off against their will by a frightened remnant of resistance fighters, royal family members, and some poor of the land. Jeremiah died a brokenhearted prophet in the

---

26. The NRSV provides a textual note with an alternate ethnic name, *Nubian*. The ancient kingdom of Nubia was located south of Egypt, in what is today Sudan. Ebed-melech is designated a *saris* in Hebrews, a title probably referring not to a physical eunuch (as in NRSV) but to a court official (as in TNIV).

27. One recalls the "coincidences" that occur in the book of Esther, witnessing to the presence of the unseen God who sees all things and accomplishes his purposes (Esth 4:12-14; 6:1-2).

land of Egypt, where Israel's national history had begun in bondage nearly a millennium before. What an ironic and tragic end for prophet and people.

EXILE IN EGYPT

According to chapters 43–44, after the destruction of Jerusalem, Jeremiah prophesied to the Jewish refugees in Egypt (Jer 43:4–7). We don't really know how long he lived in Egypt, nor do we know how he died. According to one Jewish tradition, Egyptian Jews in Tahpanhes stoned him to death. This is probably the source for the church father Tertullian's brief reference to Jeremiah being stoned.[28] If this be so, it was a rocky end to a rocky road for Jeremiah. Another rabbinic tradition ascribes a less violent ending in which Jeremiah dies of natural causes in Babylon.[29] At any rate, his ministry lasted at least forty years, making Jeremiah one of the longest-serving prophets in the OT, with possibly only Isaiah ministering longer.

JEREMIAH THE PROPHET LIKE MOSES

We've earlier mentioned some similarities between Jeremiah's call and that of other prophets. The figure that looms largest in Jeremiah's call is Moses.[30] The fact that Moses felt totally inadequate for the task because he was "slow of speech and tongue" (Exod 4:10) is echoed in Jeremiah's reluctance: "I do not know how to speak" (Jer 1:6). The single most important connection between these men, however, lies in Jeremiah's consciousness of his prophetic commission *as a successor to Moses*. In the book of Deuteronomy, Yahweh promises Moses, "I will raise up for them a prophet like you from among their people, and I will put my words in his mouth. He will tell them everything I command him" (Deut 18:18). Jeremiah

---

28. Tertullian, *Scorpiace*, 8.
29. Seder 'Olam Rabbah 26.
30. Lundbom, *Prophet Like Moses*, 2.

envisioned himself as a prophet like Moses. It is no accident that many passages in the book of Jeremiah reverberate with phraseology from the book of Deuteronomy. Most notably, Jeremiah's emphasis on the normative role of the Mosaic covenant and the urgency to reinstate it through heartfelt repentance and observance of its stipulations is deeply rooted in Deuteronomy.[31] In addition, the litany of complaints against Moses in the Sinai narratives find their counterpart in Jeremiah's complaints about the unrelenting criticism of his opponents. In short, both prophets endure major disappointments, none more poignant than the circumstances of their deaths: Moses, denied divine permission to set foot in the promised land, died on Mt. Nebo; Jeremiah probably died down in Egypt, far from the land he loved.

JEREMIAH AMONG THE PROPHETS

Taken together, prophetic call narratives afford a valuable insight into God's modus operandi. None of the individuals summoned into service as Yahweh's spokesperson actively expected or sought the office. The call comes "out of the blue" and rocks the world of the recipient. The last thing Moses expected out on the backside of the Sinai desert was a summons to go to Pharaoh and demand that the Hebrews be liberated. After all, he was an escaped felon and could scarcely expect anything other than arrest and execution for disloyalty and murder. Young Samuel in effect had a foster father because his mother, Hannah, after weaning Samuel, entrusted him to the care of the high priest Eli (1 Sam 1:24–28). For his part, Eli was a delinquent father who failed to discipline his own sons for egregious sins. A dysfunctional foster family is hardly the expected home environment for a great prophet (1 Sam 2:12–17, 22–25). Amos made no pretensions to position or prestige when he was

---

31. "The book Jeremiah read developed into the book that Jeremiah wrote. Just as Deuteronomy *repreached* the message of Moses to a people who had lost touch with Moses, so Jeremiah *repreached* the message of Deuteronomy to a people who had drifted from its moorings." Peterson, *Run with the Horses*, 121 (italics his).

called: "I was neither a prophet nor the disciple of a prophet, but I was a shepherd, and I also took care of sycamore-fig trees. But the LORD took me from tending the flock, and said to me, 'Go, prophesy to my people Israel'" (Amos 7:14–15). Hosea experienced a painful divorce as a prelude to preaching to an unfaithful nation (Hos 1–3). Ezekiel was a Zadokite priest living in a refugee camp with Jewish exiles along the Chebar canal in Babylon (modern Iraq). Suddenly, Yahweh summoned him to be his prophet in his thirtieth year, the year he would ordinarily have begun to exercise his priestly duties in the Jerusalem temple were he still there (Ezek 1:1–3). Ezekiel was taken totally by surprise, since he assumed that living in a pagan land rendered him unclean and "beyond the pale." Quite the contrary, the holy God of Israel was very much present in this foreign, idolatrous land. In short, Ezekiel was called to proclaim the ongoing responsibility of the people of God to live holy lives in the midst of an unholy land. Ironically, in his prophesying, Ezekiel performed his priestly role after all.

The same pattern of unmerited and unexpected grace bestowed upon those summoned to proclaim the word of Yahweh reappears in the NT. The Apostle Paul immediately comes to mind. Near the end of his missionary career, Paul looks back over his life as an apostle and can only marvel at God's grace and mercy. Though "once a blasphemer and a persecutor and a violent man," he was called into service by the Lord Jesus (1 Tim 1:13–14). Though Paul considers himself the foremost sinner that Christ saved, he offers praise that God used him to serve as an example to other sinners (1 Tim 1:15–17). Other Pauline passages pick up on this theme (1 Cor 15:8–10; Gal 1:13–24; Phil 3:5–11).

The offices of prophet and apostle are daunting assignments. But so is being a witness for Christ. Followers of the Lamb (Rev 14:4b) must necessarily deal with fear and nagging inadequacies. How could it be otherwise? Thankfully, one of the regular features of prophetic call experiences is a word of divine assurance. "I will be with you" rings in the spiritual ears of those summoned to speak in his name. In Isaiah's visionary experience, a seraph with searing coals cauterizes his unclean lips (Isa 6:6–7). Only then does he step forward and say, "Here am I, send me!" Ezekiel, also in a visionary trance, is commanded to eat a scroll containing divinely dictated words for the house of Israel (Ezek 3:1–3). Like Jeremiah, Yahweh forewarns Ezekiel about the unwillingness of his listeners to heed his preaching. But no matter, Yahweh assures the prophet, "I will make your forehead like the hardest stone, harder than flint. Do not be afraid of them or terrified by them, though they are a rebellious house" (Ezek 3:9). Remarkably, Ezekiel never wavers.

Here is a truth on which the people of God in every age must absolutely depend. When God calls us to step up and speak in his name, he will strengthen us for the task. One is reminded of Jesus's promise to his apostles: "For I will give you words and a wisdom that none of your adversaries will be able to resist or contradict" (Luke 21:15). But this doesn't apply only to apostles. Addressing rank-and-file believers, Peter urges his readers, "'Do not fear their threats; and do not be frightened.' But in your hearts revere Christ as Lord. Always be prepared to give an answer to anyone who asks you to give the reason for the hope that you have" (1 Pet 3:14–15). The Apostle Paul speaks for all who seek to faithfully follow the Lord: "That is why, for Christ's sake, I delight in weaknesses, in insults, in hardships, in persecutions, in difficulties. For when I am weak, then I am strong" (2 Cor 12:10). Jeremiah embodied this truth, and so should we.

2

The Temple Sermon

No sermon preached by Jeremiah ever struck such a raw nerve in the popular psyche as his temple sermon. Epitomizing his mission and message, this sermon conveniently serves as a summary of his preaching.[1] The fact that it is narrated twice (Jer 7 and 26) indicates its importance. Especially eye-opening is the second retelling because it focuses on the audience reaction. The temple courtyard erupts with boiling rage as the priests, prophets, and people cry out, "You must die!" (26:8). Where did that come from? My aim in this chapter is twofold: 1) to understand why Jeremiah's message elicited such anger, and 2) to discuss its theological significance for our day.

OCCASION AND SETTING

Chapter 26 places the sermon "at the beginning of the reign of King Jehoiakim" (v. 1), about 609 BC. In the wake of Josiah's tragic death at Megiddo, Judah became an Egyptian vassal state. Pharaoh Neco II deposed Josiah's son Jehoahaz after only three months and

---

1. "Perhaps the clearest and most formidable statement we have of the basic themes of the Jeremiah tradition." Brueggemann, *To Pluck Up*, 74.

replaced him with another son, Jehoiakim.[2] This new political reality looms in the background of Jeremiah's sermon. The setting is the gate (7:2) and courtyard (26:2) of the Jerusalem temple, called "the LORD's house."

Can we be more precise about the occasion? Yahweh instructs Jeremiah to position himself in a strategic location in order to maximize the audience. In other words, Jeremiah gets top billing in prime time. Furthermore, one gets the impression that this was not an ordinary day but a larger than usual assembly, such as occurred during the annual pilgrimage festivals, Pesach (Passover), Shavuot (Weeks), and Succoth (Tabernacles or Booths). Nothing in Jeremiah's sermon explicitly identifies the precise occasion, but he does indict his listeners for failing to keep the stipulations of the Sinai covenant, actually quoting from commandments five through ten of the Ten Commandments and summarizing the first three commandments about exclusive loyalty to Yahweh (Jer 7:8–11). Since later Jewish tradition held that Moses received the Ten Commandments during Shavuot, some suggest this as a clue to the timing of the temple sermon. Admittedly, such a connection is tenuous. Pesach, being the festival connected with the national birth of Israel, would also have been an appropriate occasion. Others suggest the fall festival of Succoth. Certainty eludes us.

In the previous chapter, I discussed an episode that took place five years after the temple sermon, when Jehoiakim proclaimed a public fast and large numbers of people flooded into the temple precincts (Jer 36). Perhaps Jehoiakim had issued an earlier fast in light of the crisis following Josiah's death and Jehoahaz's banishment to Egypt. At the outset of Jehoiakim's reign, a jittery Judah needed some assurance that everything would be okay. This provides a plausible explanation for the occasion.

Let me add an additional perspective. Regardless of whether the occasion was one of the pilgrimage festivals or a publicly

---

2. I can only speculate on the reason, but probably Jehoahaz sought to reestablish Judean independence from Egyptian control. At any rate, Neco deposed him and appointed another son as regent. The fact that Neco levied tribute on Judah and changed Eliakim's name to Jehoiakim reflects this new subservient relationship (2 Kgs 23:30–35).

announced fast, Jeremiah's presence and preaching at the temple gate may be rooted in the temple liturgy. Evidence from the Psalms suggests that during the days of the First Temple corporate worship involved an entrance liturgy.[3] That is, a priest (or prophet) exhorted worshipers who sought entrance into the temple courtyard to examine their behavior before standing in the presence of a holy God. Psalms 15 and 24 seem to reflect just such a liturgy in the form of an antiphonal hymn:

Participants and Action	Psalm 15	Psalm 24
Worshipers' request for admittance	LORD, who may dwell in your sanctuary? Who may live on your holy mountain?	Who may ascend the mountain of the LORD? Who may stand in his holy place?
Priestly (or prophetic) response	Those whose walk is blameless, who do what is righteous, who speak the truth from their hearts . . .	Those who have clean hands and a pure heart, who do not put their trust in an idol or swear by a false god.
Worshipers and priests sing in unison	Whoever does these things will never be shaken.	Such is the generation of those who seek him, who seek your face, God of Jacob.

In other words, a time of introspection and self-examination preceded communal worship—a practice still observed in Christian liturgy.[4] Going further, Jeremiah, who was both a priest and a prophet, might have adapted this liturgy as the perfect opportunity to confront his audience and call them to repentance. While this suggestion falls short of proof, it offers a plausible setting for Jeremiah's memorable message.

3. "Jeremiah was clearly familiar with the Psalter, which was the Temple songbook. When completed, the Psalter comprised five songbooks, but many Psalms in Books I–II had already been written and were being sung in Jeremiah's time." Lundbom, *Prophet Like Moses*, 98.

4. The *Book of Common Prayer* includes this exhortation before the Eucharist: "Examine your lives and conduct by the rule of God's commandments . . ." (317).

In the previous chapter, we discussed a confrontation between King Jehoiakim and the prophet Jeremiah (Jer 36). That clash had its roots in this incendiary sermon, right at the beginning of Jehoiakim's tenure. Not only did Jeremiah's sermon ignite a firestorm of public criticism, it initiated a state of belligerency between king and prophet. Let's delve into it further and follow the flow of Jeremiah's homily.

OUTLINE OF JEREMIAH'S TEMPLE SERMON (JER 7)

- Narrative superscription: Divine commission (vv. 1–2)
- Introduction: Messenger formula (v. 3a)
- Exhortation: Reform your ways and your actions (vv. 3b–7)
- Warning: Stop trusting in slogans and get serious about Sinai (vv. 8–11)
- Warning: Remember Shiloh (vv. 12–15)

SUMMARY

In one skillful stroke, Jeremiah cuts right to the heart of what it means to be God's holy people and, at the same time, cuts the feet out from under his listeners, who think the God of Sinai will protect them in their hour of need. Having fled to the place of supreme safety, the sacred space hallowed by Yahweh's name, they were in fact standing at ground zero! Once again, the irony is palpable. Here they were invoking Yahweh's protection, all the while leading lives completely out of sync with his purpose for their lives. No words of comfort and consolation from this prophet! No sugarcoating and no holding back (Jer 26:2). He rings down upon them the ultimate covenant curse for disobedience and, in effect, utters a solemn "Ichabod" over the whole site and its hypocritical worshipers. Too bad we don't have a YouTube video of the occasion. This was a massive bombshell.

THE TEMPLE SERMON

ANALYSIS OF THE SERMON

So what did Jeremiah actually say? His main point is unmistakable: the actions and deeds of the audience are irreconcilable with the meaning of the temple as the dwelling place of "the LORD of hosts, the God of Israel." True worshipers must be committed to the supreme summons of the Sinai covenant: "Be holy, for I the LORD your God am holy" (Lev 19:2). In fact, they were horrible. Mere participation in the temple liturgies and rituals cannot mask this glaring disconnect.

Covenant Lawsuit

Jeremiah essentially indicts the nation for noncompliance with the Sinai covenant. Like a prosecuting attorney, he enters into evidence three exhibits of covenant violations: oppression of the powerless, murder, and disloyalty to their great overlord, the God of Sinai (7:5–7). These transgressions are just the tip of the iceberg. In verses 8–9, Jeremiah expands the scope of offenses by ticking off commandments five through eight and concluding with commandment one from the Ten Commandments. In short, they are in complete noncompliance and have absolutely no mitigating circumstances behind which to hide.[5]

Worth noting before passing on is Jeremiah's incorporation of a familiar feature of prophetic judgment oracles, namely, the covenant lawsuit.[6] In this regard, Jeremiah reflects his indebtedness to his prophetic predecessors, especially the northern prophet

---

5. "His message was that Yahweh had declared holy war against a people in gross violation of the Sinai covenant." Lundbom, *Prophet Like Moses*, 51.

6. "Judgment oracles typically consist of an address, an accusation, and a judicial sentence. Their content derives from the Mosaic covenant: if the nation reneges on its covenant promises to obey Torah, God's integrity guarantees his punishment, but not before due warnings." Waltke, *Old Testament Theology*, 830. For further discussion of the Sinai covenant as an adaptation of an Ancient Near Eastern suzerainty treaty, see Helyer, *Yesterday*, 149–57.

Hosea.[7] Hosea presents an indictment of his eighth-century contemporaries in language strikingly similar to that of Jeremiah:

> Hear the word of the LORD, you Israelites, because the LORD has a charge to bring against you who live in the land. There is no faithfulness, no love [NRSV: loyalty], no acknowledgment of God in the land. There is only cursing, lying and murder, stealing and adultery; they break all bounds, and bloodshed follows bloodshed. (Hos 4:1–2)

This kind of covenant lawsuit language also appears in Amos (2:4–8; 4:1–12), Isaiah (1:2–31), and Micah (6:1–8).

Like an alarm bell, Jeremiah's sermon alerts the audience to a security breach. The listeners have a faulty theological understanding leading to a misplaced confidence in the safety of the temple. Jeremiah reiterates a current slogan designed to allay the anxious fears of those who crowded into the temple complex: "This is the temple of the LORD, the temple of the LORD, the temple of the LORD" (7:4). Notice how the threefold repetition sounds like a mantra with magical powers to protect from danger, demonstrating how superstition had eroded faith in Yahweh. As in the days of Isaiah, the people of Judah act like pagans: "They are full of superstitions from the East; they practice divination like the Philistines and clasp hands with pagans" (Isa 2:6).

What accounts for this mistaken sense of security? Two factors were at play. One was a David-Zion theology arising from prophetic oracles promising an everlasting Davidic dynasty reigning on Mt. Zion. Nathan the prophet utters this word of Yahweh: "Your house and your kingdom will endure forever before me; your throne will be established forever" (2 Sam 7:12–16).

An oracle like this certainly conveys a sense of inviolability and invincibility. Passages from the psalmody of Israel proclaiming the steadfast nature of Davidic kingship and the impregnability of Zion reinforce this conviction. Thus Yahweh swears, "I have installed my king on Zion, my holy mountain" (Ps 2:6; cf. 89:19–37;

---

7. "Early Jeremiah preaching, both in its language and ideas, betrays a substantial debt to this [Hosea's] preaching." Lundbom, *Prophet Like Moses*, 89.

The Temple Sermon

132:11–18), and "the LORD has chosen Zion, he has desired it for his dwelling, saying, 'This is my resting place for ever and ever; here I will sit enthroned, for I have desired it'" (Ps 132:13–14).[8]

A second contributing factor arose from the enduring memory of an event that occurred in Jerusalem just over a century before Jeremiah's day—the miraculous deliverance of Zion from the Assyrian siege of Sennacherib (ca. 701 BC). When all seemed lost and the city braced for an inevitable breach and bloodbath, Yahweh intervened by destroying 185,000 soldiers in one night.[9] Sennacherib was forced to withdraw and Jerusalem was spared (2 Kgs 18:13—19:36; Isa 36–47). This last-minute reprieve seemed to verify the invulnerability of Mt. Zion and the dynasty that ruled from its heights. One way or another Yahweh would see to it that his holy house on his holy mount would never suffer desecration or destruction. The mindset of the worried worshipers who mouth the mantra, "This is the temple of the LORD," climaxes in the slogan, "We are safe!" (Jer 7:10). Jeremiah has the chutzpah to say, wrong!

So what's wrong with this theological sloganeering? In short, it fails to understand the contingent nature of David-Zion theology. It conveniently ignores the fact that the Sinai covenant conditions the physical continuance of the Davidic dynasty and the temple on Mt. Zion upon covenant obedience. This was already revealed to Solomon: "But if you or your descendants turn away from me . . . then I will cut Israel off from the land that I have given them and will reject this temple I have consecrated for my Name . . . This temple will become a heap of rubble" (1 Kgs 9:6–8). This is precisely Jeremiah's point: the people are in total noncompliance, and the ultimate sanction for disobedience looms over the nation.[10] In fact, things are so bad, says Jeremiah, that Yahweh's

---

8. On the location and theological significance of Mt. Zion, see Helyer, *Mountaintop Theology*, 130–37.

9. This judgment recalls the tenth plague on Egypt, in which "at midnight the LORD struck down all the firstborn in Egypt" (Exod 12:29).

10. "For a people to boast in the glory of the past, and to deny the secret that made the past, is to perish." Morgan, *Studies*, 19.

house has become "a den of robbers" (Jer 7:11). Ominously, Jeremiah utters this word of Yahweh: "But I have been watching!" (Jer 7:11). These words bring us back to Jeremiah's opening vision of the almond tree: "I am watching to see that my word is fulfilled" (Jer 1:11). The lawsuit is uncontestable; the defendant is guilty as charged. Only two questions remain. Will Judah repent, and, if not, when will Yahweh carry out the sentence?

History Lesson

Jeremiah realizes that accusing his listeners of covenant violations will be insufficient to shake them out of their spiritual stupor—drastic measures are required. The occasion of a national assembly in the temple precincts provides the perfect setting in which to capture their undivided attention. What follows is a history lesson that shakes them to the core.

Jeremiah, speaking in first person as Yahweh himself, summons his audience to make a mental pilgrimage back to the days when Yahweh's dwelling place was Shiloh, some four hundred years earlier.[11] "Go now to the place in Shiloh where I first made a dwelling for my Name, and see what I did to it because of the wickedness of my people Israel" (7:12).[12] Jeremiah recalls a painful memory in Hebrew history: the utter desolation of the Shiloh sanctuary, the capture of the ark of the covenant, and the death of the high priest Eli and his two wicked sons, Hophni and Phinehas (1 Sam 4). It was one of the darkest days of Israel's history. With this episode fresh in their minds, Jeremiah, in the name of Yahweh, announces the unthinkable: "Therefore what I did to Shiloh I will now do to the house that bears my Name, the temple you trust in, the place I gave to you and your ancestors. I will thrust you from my presence, just as I did all your fellow Israelites, the people of Ephraim"

---

11. "Jeremiah attempted to shock his people into a recognition of this obvious but avoided truth by sending them on a field trip to Shiloh." Peterson, *Run with the Horses*, 68.

12. Shiloh lay less than twenty miles due north of Jerusalem just off the ancient ridge route in the tribal allotment of Ephraim.

(7:14-15). The last clause of Jeremiah's pronouncement refers to a much more recent disaster—the destruction and deportation of the northern tribes of Israel in 722 BC. The impact of this utterance registered a nine on the Richter scale. An emotionally fragile people, clinging to a false hope, must come to grips with a fearful reality: the jig is up and judgment day looms. The only question is, What will they do now? Yahweh informs Jeremiah that he has not yet slammed shut the door; a small opening remains. "Perhaps they will listen and each will turn from their evil ways. Then I will relent and not inflict on them the disaster I was planning because of the evil they have done" (Jer 26:3). If they meet this condition, Yahweh promises to let them dwell in the promised land (7:7).

Audience Reaction

So what happens? The listeners respond with rage: "The priests and the prophets and all the people seized him and said, 'You must die!'" (26:8). A public execution was about to take place, and doubtless it would have had not word of this public disturbance in the temple courtyard come to the attention of the officials of Judah meeting nearby. They intervene and inquire into the cause of the uproar at the New Gate entrance. In an ad hoc judicial setting, the priests and prophets enter a formal charge against Jeremiah: "This man should be sentenced to death because he has prophesied against this city" (Jer 26:11). In short, they charge Jeremiah with high treason, a capital offense.

Jeremiah's Defense

The officials allow Jeremiah to answer his accusers. Once again, he has a public platform from which to plead his case, and he does not back down or beg for mercy. His defense consists of three primary points:

- He claims to be an authentic messenger of Yahweh. He does not speak on his own authority but in the name of Yahweh, the God of Israel and Judah.

- His message calling for repentance is contingent. If the people respond positively and amend their behavior, Yahweh will change his mind and rescind his verdict of disaster upon Jerusalem and its temple. The destiny of both lies in the hands of the people.

- He rests his case with the people. If, however, they go ahead and put him to death, they will only add to their collective guilt.

Jeremiah's courageous defense strikes home with the officials and people. They are well aware of the esteemed status of Yahweh's personal spokespersons. Towering figures like Samuel, Elijah, Elisha, and Nathan commanded respect and served as advisors to kings. Though Jeremiah's message was offensive, they grudgingly conceded that it was not unprecedented in Hebrew prophecy. In fact, some of the graybeards in the audience came forward to remind them that in the days of King Hezekiah, Micah of Moresheth had prophesied a similar fate for Jerusalem.[13] The elders acknowledged that Hezekiah did not put Micah to death; in fact, the people entreated Yahweh for mercy, and he heard their plea and changed his mind. Then, in a telling conclusion, the elders warn the audience that if they put Jeremiah to death, they will certainly bring disaster upon themselves. That carries the day. The people of Judah and Jerusalem were not prepared to risk all by snuffing out the life of a peevish prophet.

At this point in the narrative, Jeremiah (or a later editor) inserts an account of a contemporary prophet, Uriah of Kiriath-jearim, who prophesied against Jerusalem and paid for it with his life. In fact, it was none other than King Jehoiakim who did away with Uriah (Jer 26:20–23). The extreme peril Jeremiah faced could hardly be greater. Thankfully, Jeremiah had a friend in high places or he too would have perished. Ahikam son of Shaphan, a royal

---

13. Jer 26:18 quoting Mic 3:12.

official, intervened and granted Jeremiah protective custody (Jer 26:24), another instance in which Yahweh kept his promise to Jeremiah (1:18–19).[14]

Though Jeremiah survived to prophesy another day, King Jehoiakim became a personal enemy from that day forward. As for a majority of the priests and prophets, they steadfastly opposed Jeremiah and vilified him as a national traitor. We will have more to say later about the self-proclaimed prophets who caused such anguish for Jeremiah.

JEREMIAH AND JESUS: PROPHETS OF DOOM

When reading about Jeremiah's temple sermon, one hears echoes of another confrontation in the temple area in which listeners reacted with rage. Of course, it was the Second Temple, not the First, and it was Jesus, not Jeremiah, who struck a raw nerve. The gospels narrate multiple occasions in which Jesus preached in the temple courtyards, and the similarities to Jeremiah's preaching are striking. In fact, many of Jesus's contemporaries actually thought he might be Jeremiah come back from the dead.[15]

All four Gospels narrate an occasion in which Jesus confronted the temple authorities in the temple courts. The confrontation took place during Passover and thus large crowds of worshipers were present to witness it.[16] Jesus condemned the practice of

---

14. This was probably the same Ahikam who consulted with the prophet Huldah in the days of Josiah (2 Kgs 22:12, 14) and was sympathetic to Josiah's reform and Jeremiah's call for repentance. Most likely, he was also the father of Gedaliah, whom Nebuchadnezzar appointed governor of Judah after the Babylonian destruction of Jerusalem (2 Kgs 25:22). Some scholars conjecture that Ahikam had a hand in the final form of the book of Jeremiah. The name of Ahikam's father, Shaphan, appears on a bulla (a clay seal on documents) dating to the time of Jehoiakim. It was recovered by Yigal Shiloh during his Jerusalem excavations in 1982 (Schneider, "Six Biblical Signatures").

15. "When Jesus came to the region of Caesarea Philippi, he asked his disciples, 'Who do people say the Son of Man is?' They replied, 'Some say John the Baptist; others say Elijah; and still others, Jeremiah or one of the prophets'" (Matt 16:13–14).

16. The Synoptic Gospels place the episode during the last week of Jesus's

selling sacrificial animals in the temple courts, a practice probably owing to convenience.[17] He also drove out the moneychangers who converted local and foreign currency into the temple shekel (at considerable profit). What is especially striking is the fact that Jesus justified his actions by quoting both Isaiah and Jeremiah: "Is it not written: 'My house will be called a house of prayer for all nations'? But you have made it 'a den of robbers'" (Mark 11:17; cf. Isa 56:7 and Jer 7:11). Jesus makes the same point Jeremiah had made six centuries earlier: the temple now serves as a safe haven for evildoers. Such travesty cannot continue, and Jesus's symbolic action of cursing the fig tree on the second day of Passion Week (Mark 11:12-14) foreshadows divine punishment upon the nation and its temple because the fig tree functioned as a symbol of the nation of Israel in Second Temple Judaism. Jeremiah made the same point in his day using a linen belt (Jer 13), a clay jar (Jer 19), a basket of bad figs (Jer 24), and a yoke and crossbars (Jer 27). We will look at these symbolic actions in more detail in the next chapter.

The reaction of the religious leaders to Jesus's actions in the temple courtyards matches that of the priests and prophets of Jeremiah's day. "The chief priests and the teachers of the law heard this and began looking for a way to kill him, for they feared him, because the whole crowd was amazed at his teaching" (Mark 11:18). Jesus, like Jeremiah, escapes their wrath on this occasion. Unlike Jeremiah, however, Jesus doesn't retire from the temple area; he returns daily until his time comes to be handed over to the chief priests and the scribes (Mark 10:33; cf. John 12:30-32; 13:1).

---

earthly ministry. John's Gospel places it near the beginning. Perhaps it took place both times.

17. There were public markets at the foot of the temple platform where sacrificial animals could be purchased and currency could be converted to the temple shekel. These have come to light as a result of the excavations carried out there since 1967. It was more convenient, however, for worshipers to be able to purchase animals when they were up on the temple mount itself, in the area called the court of the Gentiles. Merchants and moneychangers seized upon this to relocate their stalls to an area that should have been reserved for prayer and reflection rather than commercial transactions.

The Temple Sermon

We've already commented on the irony that Jeremiah, firstborn son of a Jerusalem priest, announced the destruction of the very temple in which his father served. In the magnificent Second Temple, the crown jewel of Herod the Great's Jerusalem, Joseph and Mary dedicated their firstborn son to the Lord and performed the purification rites required of mothers who gave birth (Luke 2:22-24; cf. Lev 12:4-8). During that time, a devout man named Simeon, guided by the Holy Spirit, took Jesus up in his arms and offered praise to God for revealing his salvation through this child. He then adds these ominous words: "This child is destined to cause the falling and the rising of many in Israel, and to be a sign that will be spoken against, so that the thoughts of many hearts will be revealed. And a sword will pierce your own soul too" (Luke 2:34-35). Jeremiah and Jesus were both destined to be an offense to many of their contemporaries.

As a twelve-year-old, Jesus appeared in the temple precincts and amazed the religious leaders with his precocious understanding (Luke 2:47). He even spoke of the temple as "my Father's house" (Luke 2:49). As an adult, however, false witnesses accused him of saying he would destroy the temple and in three days build another (Mark 14:57-59; 15:29-30).[18] According to Matthew's Gospel, he told a parable that foreshadowed divine judgment upon the city (Matt 22:7). On the day of his triumphal entry into Jerusalem, those nearby witnessed him weeping over the city and uttering a lament over its impending destruction (Luke 19:41-44). To his inner circle of disciples, however, he explicitly predicted the utter destruction of the temple such that "not one stone here will be left on another; every one will be thrown down" (Matt 24:2). On his way to Golgotha, Jesus warns the wailing women of the approaching tragedy (Luke 23:27-31). The shadow of Jeremiah's temple sermon hangs like a pall over Passion Week.

---

18. The Gospel of John clarifies that Jesus was actually speaking of his own body as a temple, and thus it was a prediction of his resurrection (John 2:21-22).

THEOLOGICAL SIGNIFICANCE OF THE TEMPLE SERMON

The temple sermon exposed a fallacy in Judah's national ideology. They assumed that Yahweh's election of the Davidic dynasty and the Jerusalem temple cult included an unbreakable promise of divine protection. As already mentioned, they failed to reckon with the proper relationship between Sinai and Zion theology. The latter does not abrogate the former. Judah may not flout the covenant obligations of Sinai and then expect Yahweh to overlook their egregious transgressions and blatant disloyalty. Accountability has conveniently disappeared from national consciousness.

Does this fascinating episode in the life of Jeremiah have theological significance for believers living in twenty-first-century America? This is a very contentious issue. Applying Jeremiah's sermon to America requires great caution. One must not assume that the United States stands in a similar covenant relationship with the Lord. Many have done so, but, in my opinion, this contributes to a flawed national ideology.[19] A reading of early American history in which George Washington essentially functions like a new Moses and the Declaration of Independence, the Constitution, and the Bill of Rights of the United States assume virtual canonical status is highly questionable.[20] Just because "In God We Trust" is printed on our currency and stamped on our coins does not confirm our status as a new covenant people of God. Nor is it theologically tenable to view George Washington's inaugural address and prayer on April 30, 1789, as evidence that the United States is in a covenant relationship with God.

---

19. Many conservative Protestants have been staunch supporters of this view. See, e.g., Marshall and Manuel, *Light and the Glory* (1977); LaHaye, *Faith of Our Founding Fathers* (1994); and Robertson, *America's Dates with Destiny* (1986). Perhaps the most visible and vocal champion of this view is David Barton, founder of WallBuilders, an organization that seeks to defend America as a Christian nation. See, e.g., Barton, *America's Godly Heritage* (2009) and Barton, *Jefferson Lies* (2012). The Mormon Church, citing the Book of Mormon, holds a similar view (see 1 Nephi 12:1; 13:14; 14:2; 2 Nephi 1:5, 10; Ether 2:8).

20. See Wilsey, *American Exceptionalism*, 22.

The Temple Sermon

The primary objection to such an understanding is that the New Testament makes clear that God's new covenant people, the church, is a spiritual, transcultural, transethnic, and global community of faith (Eph 2–3; Col 3:11; 1 Pet 2:9; Rev 5:9; 7:9; 21:24–26). As such, God's chosen people live as citizens of two kingdoms, a specific kingdom of this world and the vastly more important, transcendent kingdom of Christ. These two must neither be conflated nor confused. This in short is the fundamental flaw of the Christian America thesis.[21]

To be sure, Pilgrim and Puritan theology often envisioned the voyage to the New World as a second exodus—an escaping from the oppression of Egypt (England) and a crossing of the Red Sea (the Atlantic). They also likened their settlement in America to a new conquest of Canaan. A tragic consequence of such an understanding was the equation of Native Americans with Canaanites. This helped justify the settlers' unconscionable treatment of the original inhabitants.[22] Puritan preachers proclaimed this typology from their pulpits and in their writings.[23] In so doing, they contributed to an emerging national mythology, a vision of America as "a city set on a hill."[24] But Puritan pulpiteering does not guarantee theological correctness.[25] Furthermore, it would be

---

21. A point passionately argued by Boyd, *Myth of a Christian Nation*. For a more dispassionate discussion from an academic historian who is an evangelical, see Fea, *Christian Nation?*

22. "Gradually the idea that the Indian belonged to an inferior and accursed race came to prevail, justifying the liquidation or enslavement by the colonists." Olmstead, *Religion in the United States*, 82.

23. "Through the enormous volume of Puritan writings in the form of sermons, books, pamphlets, newspapers, letters and so on, Puritan thought spread from New England to the Middle and Southern Colonies as well as to the western hinterlands." Wilsey, *American Exceptionalism*, 40.

24. A phrase first used by John Winthrop, the first governor of the Massachusetts Bay Colony. See Winthrop, "Modell of Christian Charity," 40. President Ronald Reagan most notably rehabilitated the phrase and President George W. Bush articulated, if not its exact wording, at least its spirit.

25. "Unlike Israel, we have no biblical or empirical reason to believe God ever intended to be king over America in any unique sense." Boyd, *Myth of a Christian Nation*, 148.

a mistake to assume that a majority of new settlers shared this self-understanding. Many who risked the voyage and the formidable challenges of carving out a new life in the wilderness operated with a quite different vision of the new world. In fact, the primary impetus for English colonization of the New World was not religious but economic and social.[26]

More fundamentally, however, I question the hermeneutical basis of America as the new promised land. Such a thesis requires an appeal to extrabiblical authority. Ironically, the Puritan interpretation of America as the new covenant people of God undermines a basic Reformation principle so important to Puritan theology, namely, *sola Scriptura* (Scripture alone). The Puritans affirmed that Scripture, not tradition, is the final authority for faith and practice, but a Christian America typology assumes new revelation in which America becomes only the second people in history to enter into a covenant relationship with God. Let me be emphatic: there is no evidence *from the Bible itself* to support such an interpretation. One must read it into the text, a classic example of eisegesis. The Puritans were right in seeing a typological connection between Israel and the church because the New Testament makes precisely such a connection; they were wrong, however, in extending this typology to America because there is no New Testament validation for it and there is no Third Testament.

Can we, however, make a legitimate theological application of this passage to our situation as citizens of the United States of America in the twenty-first century? With caution, I believe we can. The God of Israel is the God of all nations, and all nations are responsible to render justice and righteousness. Failing this,

26. The eminent church historian Kenneth Scott Latourette, a devout Baptist, concludes, "In spite of the part which Christianity had in initiating and shaping the Thirteen Colonies, in 1750 the large majority of the white population were without a formal church connexion. It has been estimated ... that in 1750 only about five out of a hundred were members of churches. The overwhelming proportion of the settlers came to the colonies for economic or social rather than religious motives. They were mostly from the underprivileged and by migrating to the New World sought to better their financial or their social standing." Latourette, *History of Christianity*, 954. See also Olmstead, *Religion in the United States*, 40–41.

each must face the consequences of national injustice, oppression, and unrighteousness. God's providence rules the world, and in his providence, God has singularly blessed this nation. For this we give thanks. Nevertheless, we have also experienced his stern judgment for injustice and oppression. As one example, the American Civil War witnessed his "terrible swift sword" in which more than six hundred thousand lives were lost. We are still dealing with its aftermath.

Just as the people of Judah held a faulty theological understanding of their relationship with Yahweh, so too, I fear, many American Christians assume a flawed understanding of America's role in world history. What has happened is a subtle fusion of the kingdom of God and the United States of America. God and country have become indivisible and inseparable. The result is a Christianized civil religion. Such a syncretism relies on selective theological constructs drawn from the Bible, such as national election, covenantal obligation (with consequences for noncompliance), and a manifest destiny to be a beacon for Christianity and democracy—to which is often added individualism and free-market capitalism. This explicit and subliminal equation of the kingdom of God with America has generated a number of harmful consequences, not least of which is the creation of unnecessary barriers for the gospel, whether at home or abroad. This version of the gospel smacks of Americanism. "The evangelical church in America has, to a large extent, been co-opted by an American, religious version of the kingdom of the world."[27]

Operating under a Christian America self-understanding, many evangelicals sense they are losing something very dear to them. Christian America is under assault and in danger of losing her birthright, they argue; Christian values are being eroded and irretrievably lost.[28] For many evangelicals, it was unthinkable to vote for Hillary Clinton, a candidate who championed abortion rights, opposed tougher immigration policies, supported

---

27. Boyd, *Myth of a Christian Nation*, 90.

28. "Preserving what was being lost became the primary fuel propelling the so-called religious right." Daly, "Importance of Listening," 176.

the LGBTQ community, and was in favor of expanded national healthcare, stricter gun control laws, and more restrictive environmental regulations. These issues "trumped" all others for a large majority of white evangelicals.

One of the hallmarks of American presidential campaigns has been party slogans designed to rally support for their candidates. The 2016 election was a classic example as the two major political parties put forth in their campaign slogans two quite different visions of what America should be: "Stronger Together" (Hillary Clinton) and "Make America Great Again." (Donald Trump). The Trump slogan resonated with large numbers of white evangelicals. Pollsters estimate that about 81 percent of white evangelicals voted for him. No doubt the perception that America had lost ground economically and militarily and that liberal elites had hijacked the national agenda resonated with many of these voters. But what many of them heard was "Make America *Christian* Again." A majority of evangelicals yearn for a conservative president who will alter the composition of the Supreme Court and eventually overturn *Roe vs. Wade*. They also want to ban same-sex marriage and in general turn back the LGBTQ movement. In their view, only such action can save America from God's wrath. Furthermore, a conservative Supreme Court will protect Second Amendment rights, so dear to many white evangelicals. Christian colleges and universities anxiously fret about losing federal funding unless they drop behavioral standards prohibiting faculty, staff, and students from engaging in same-sex relationships and provide restrooms accessible to those who identify as transgender. To this list of concerns could be added anxiety over the influx of illegal immigrants and Muslim refugees, the threat of radical Islamic terrorism, the removal of "In God We Trust" from our currency, and the general disparagement of evangelical Christianity in the entertainment industry, mainline news media, and the public square. Consequently, many evangelicals invest enormous emotional energy (and money) into supporting political candidates and policies that are in line with a Christian America self-understanding.[29]

29. For a study of the historical background behind the 81 percent white evangelical vote for Trump, see Fea, *Believe Me*.

The Temple Sermon

I believe America would be a better place if all its citizens sought to live in accord with the gospel of Christ. What we as evangelicals need to come to grips with, however, is the reality that we are a minority living in a pluralistic, liberal democracy. In that regard, we are living in a situation much like that of the early church in the pagan world of imperial Rome. The Apostle Peter's first epistle serves as an indispensable handbook on how to live out one's faith as a minority.[30] Our primary calling as evangelicals is to present a winsome witness to the Good News of Jesus Christ. "Always be ready to make your defense to anyone who demands from you an accounting for the hope that is in you; yet do it with gentleness and reverence. Keep your conscience clear, so that, when you are maligned, those who abuse you for your good conduct in Christ may be put to shame" (1 Pet 3:15–16 NRSV).

This doesn't mean we abdicate political responsibility and participation—something not even possible for first-century believers. We live in an entirely different political situation. Whereas 1 Peter urges acceptance of the governmental status quo (2:13–17), as citizens of the United States, Christians have the obligation and right to engage in the political processes of a democratic republic, including active opposition to unjust and immoral legislation and practices. But should we not also advocate policy that works for the common good, not just the privileged few? And should not racial and social justice issues, as well as environmental concerns, be included in our political priorities? Unfortunately, these matters have not gained as much traction in evangelical circles. Evangelicals have historically championed the notion of soul liberty in matters of politics and not required adherence to a particular political party or philosophy. Currently, however, political partisanship threatens to sunder the transdenominational unity that has characterized the movement from its inception in the eighteenth century.[31]

---

30. See further Helyer, *Life and Witness of Peter*, 178–82.

31. See the insightful remarks of Mark Labberton, president of Fuller Seminary, in a speech delivered at Wheaton College, titled "Political Dealing." See also his edited volume, *Still Evangelical?*

That brings me to the dark side of the Trump slogan. It gives voice to another unspoken aspiration: "Make America *White* Again." While the majority of white evangelicals do not support a racist agenda and would vociferously deny racist attitudes, the truth is that unacknowledged racism continues to rear its ugly head within the ranks of white evangelicals. Any meaningful dialogue with our African-American Christian brothers and sisters would fully support my claim.[32] Unfortunately, little meaningful dialogue about racial issues ever takes place in white evangelical churches. The reason is painfully obvious—evangelical churches constitute one of the most segregated subgroups in America.[33] This may well constitute our single most pressing need: to exhibit *now* the glorious harmony and unity of the *not yet*, the new Jerusalem.[34]

I have no doubt touched a raw nerve among some of my fellow evangelicals. While I harbor no illusions that my arguments will win over those firmly committed to a Christian America thesis, I hope my remarks will lead some to a reconsideration.

---

32. See Labberton, "Political Dealing"; Moore, "Race in Evangelical America"; and Boyd, "Racism."

33. Brooke Hempell, senior vice president of research for the Barna Group, insists that "more than any other segment of the population, white evangelical Christians demonstrate a blindness to the struggle of their African-American brothers and sisters ... Jesus and His disciples actively sought to affirm and restore the marginalized and obliterate divisions between groups of people. Yet, our churches and ministries are still some of the most ethnically segregated institutions in the country." Quoted in Larsen, "Evangelicals in Denial." For a full discussion of this problem, see Emerson and Smith, *Divided by Faith.*

34. For some positive steps that could be taken to address this problem, see DeYoung et al., *United by Faith.*

3

Jeremiah's Symbolic Actions

Jeremiah's temple sermon is a classic example of an "in your face" approach to delivering a word from Yahweh. Positioned for maximum exposure, Jeremiah ignited a firestorm in the temple courtyard by announcing the impending destruction of city and temple and a deportation of Judah's citizens, crushing all hope for a continuing national existence. That message got the audience's attention. But how do you top that? Having fired off his big cannon, how can Jeremiah follow up with messages that connect with an antagonistic audience? As it turns out, Jeremiah has a bag of rhetorical techniques by which to capture attention, even from his most hostile detractors. This chapter focuses on one of his most effective and versatile methods, namely, symbolic actions.

PROPHECY AND SYMBOLIC ACTIONS

So what are symbolic actions? In the context of Hebrew prophecy, they refer to actions that nonverbally convey Yahweh's message. Scholars use the term *sign-acts* to designate this kind of communication. The prophet may elect to accompany the action with verbal explanation, but what is acted out usually speaks for itself. One might think of symbolic actions as acted parables or object lessons.

39

The Life and Witness of Jeremiah

Another useful analogy is pantomime or street theater.[1] It requires little reflection to appreciate the effectiveness of symbolic actions. They connect with listeners because human beings are hardwired to respond to action and movement. Any preacher knows what happens if someone enters the sanctuary during a sermon and walks all the way to the front to sit down. The speaker must now recapture the attention of the audience because just about everyone in the congregation has momentarily been distracted by the newcomer whose arrival generates a multiplicity of subliminal questions in the minds of the observers. Savvy preachers initiate activity of their own in order to regain the audience's transitory attention span. Hebrew prophets were adept at capturing attention by what they did. As it turns out, Jeremiah was among the best at this technique. In this regard, only Ezekiel outperformed him. I would have to award the Oscar for Best Symbolic Action to Ezekiel—he was simply off the charts! His acting out the impending siege of Jerusalem by living on a subsistence diet for over a year—taking in just enough food and water to stay alive—left him looking like an emaciated Holocaust survivor and shocked observers (Ezek 4).

Symbolic actions fall generally into two categories: spontaneous and planned. As the name implies, spontaneous symbolic actions are not thought out in advance; they are on-the-spot reactions that speak louder than words. A classic example occurs when Saul, after his second failure to obey explicit divine instructions, tries to win back Samuel's approval. After delivering a devastating rejection of Saul's kingship, Samuel turns to leave. Saul, in desperation, reaches out to grasp Samuel's robe in hopes of changing his mind. In so doing, Samuel's robe tears. Samuel delivers an unrehearsed explanation that leaves no doubt about the divine verdict: "The Lord has torn the kingdom of Israel from you today, and has given it to one of your neighbors—to one better than you" (1 Sam 15:28).

---

1. See further Helyer, *Yesterday*, 274–77.

As an example of a premeditated symbolic action similar to the abovementioned spontaneous action, consider the story of Ahijah the prophet. Near the end of Solomon's reign, Ahijah the Shilonite meets Jeroboam, a highly placed government official in charge of forced labor under Solomon, as he is leaving Jerusalem (1 Kgs 11:29–39). One can be sure Ahijah carefully planned this meeting. Ahijah is wearing a new robe, and when the two of them are alone in the countryside, he suddenly takes off his robe and tears it into twelve pieces. Needless to say, he has Jeroboam's attention! He then invites Jeroboam to take ten pieces for himself. The interpretive word makes it crystal clear what Yahweh intends: "See, I am going to tear the kingdom out of Solomon's hand and give you ten tribes. But for the sake of my servant David and the city of Jerusalem, which I have chosen out of all the tribes of Israel, he will have one tribe" (1 Kgs 11:31–32).

JEREMIAH'S SYMBOLIC ACTIONS

Jeremiah is a classic practitioner of the art of symbolic actions. Each captures the attention of the audience by virtue of what is acted out. After his temple sermon, Jeremiah is both a celebrity and a pariah. His symbolic actions ensure that his grim message, appalling to his listeners, remains fixed in their consciousness. Lacking the power of social media, such as politicians and celebrities wield today, Jeremiah "stays on message" by a series of effective symbolic actions accompanied by his interpretations.

The Linen Belt: Airing Out Dirty Laundry

The first recorded symbolic action performed by Jeremiah occurs in chapter 13. Simple but effective, this sign-act did not take place in a single moment but unfolded over a period of several months. Therein lies its lasting impact.

Component Parts

In order to understand what's going on in this symbolic action, several interpretive issues need sorting. First, what was it that Jeremiah was ordered to purchase and wear? The Hebrew word translated as "linen belt" (TNIV), "linen loincloth" (NRSV), or "linen girdle" (KJV) refers to a luxury item worn around the waist by kings or priests. Some interpreters think that the linen belt is actually worn next to the body like underwear. Thus the NET translation reads "linen underwear" and the GNB has "linen shorts." One gets the impression, however, that by wearing this accessory Jeremiah drew others' attention to it, which would not be the case if it were underwear.

Second, the point of the symbolic action resides in the visibly altered condition of the linen belt. Initially, passersby could not help noticing Jeremiah's stylish apparel. Although Jeremiah was from a priestly family, there's no indication in the text that he actually served as a priest. But he probably was trained as a priestly scribe and that may have qualified him to wear such a linen belt. At any rate, his new belt attracted attention. In our contemporary culture, one can imagine the offhand comment, "Hey, Jeremiah, pretty cool threads!" That was the intended audience response. The explicit command "do not let it touch water" also plays a role in the meaning of the action. After a while, the linen belt needs laundering, but Jeremiah is prohibited from washing it. The newness fades and people begin to notice its less appealing appearance.

After a further unspecified period of time, part two of the symbolic action unfolds. Yahweh commands Jeremiah to go to the "Euphrates" (NRSV) or "Perath" (TNIV) and hide the linen belt in "a crevice of the rocks" (Jer 13:4). This raises two more exegetical questions. First, is this real or imaginary? Second, where is the place Jeremiah hid the linen belt?

The first question arises because, at face value, the symbolic action involves both considerable time and distance to complete. In my view, the action described is real, not visionary. Prophetic literature usually gives clear indications of visionary experiences, and this passage contains none of the usual markers (cf., e.g., Jer 1:11–13; 24:1–10; Ezek 1, et al.). It reads like a straightforward narration of something that happened in real time.

As to the place the linen belt was hidden, there is less certainty. The Hebrew place name *Perath*, in other passages, refers to the Euphrates River, running through ancient Assyria and Babylonia, modern Iraq (Gen 15:8; Deut 1:7; Josh 1:4; 2 Sam 8:3). Many interpreters, however, identify the site as Ain Fara, a spring rising just two and a half miles to the east and slightly north of Anathoth. The advantage of the latter location is its proximity and appropriateness given its rocky cliffs as opposed to the typical soil embankments found along the Euphrates. It would not take Jeremiah long to hike down to Ain Fara and find a rocky crevice alongside the wadi in which to deposit the linen belt.[2] A difficulty with the Euphrates identification is the great distance and time required to carry out the assignment. It's about a 350-mile trek one way to the Euphrates. Given that Jeremiah was later told to retrieve the linen belt many days later, this entailed two round trips totaling about 1,400 miles and several months of traveling. No wonder many have concluded this is more than can realistically be supposed.

In my opinion, however, this is precisely what did happen. The long distance and time lapse do not rule out the Euphrates. For example, Ezekiel performed a symbolic action spanning just over a year (Ezek 4–5), and the book of Jeremiah implies that couriers regularly made this journey following a well-traveled route (Jer 29:1–32). It should also be noted that at Carchemish, on the Euphrates River, there are some rock cliffs that could have served as a hiding place for the belt. Furthermore, the extended time away from Jerusalem actually adds extra impact to his action by surprising the observers with a quite different-looking linen belt. Finally, even those who prefer Ain Fara admit a probable allusion to the Euphrates inasmuch as Babylon historically functions as the agent of Judah's humiliation and degradation. In my opinion, the *Perath*

---

2. I've actually made this hike from the area of Anathoth to Ain Fara in January when there was abundant water flowing through the wadi. There are many steep cliff faces and caves in this region.

of Jeremiah 13:14 refers to the Euphrates River, an apropos hiding place in light of the overall meaning of the symbolic action.

Meaning of the Symbolic Act

That brings me to the interpretation of this symbolic act. Commentators agree that the "ruined" and "completely useless" linen belt represents Judah and Jerusalem. Jeremiah's explanatory word makes it quite clear that Yahweh has determined "to ruin the pride of Judah and the great pride of Jerusalem" (Jer 13:9). It is, however, the final interpretive word that imparts such poignancy and tragedy to the symbolic action. "'For as a belt is bound around the waist, so I bound the whole house of Israel and the whole house of Judah to me,' declares the Lord, 'to be my people for my renown and praise and honor. But they have not listened'" (Jer 13:11). Alas, like Jeremiah's linen belt, the people of Judah are ruined. Though the text does not explicitly say this, I think it likely Jeremiah wears his formerly brand-new linen belt, now quite grungy, about town. Onlookers get it. Their dirty laundry is being aired out on a daily basis. The good-for-nothing linen belt is a constant rebuke of the Judeans' moral and spiritual condition. What does one do with such a ruined garment? Throw it away. That's precisely what Yahweh intends to do with the Judeans. "All Judah is taken into exile, wholly taken into exile" (Jer 13:19). In short, Jeremiah's linen belt reinforces the famous temple sermon in a visual and unforgettable way. The irony is palpable: the very people who were called to be a glory to God have, by the greatness of their iniquity, brought only shame upon themselves (Jer 13:11, 22, 26–27). Judah can't shift the blame; she alone is responsible for her appalling spiritual decay. Because "they have not listened" (Jer 13:11), they are now "completely useless" (Jer 13:7).

Jeremiah's Celibacy: A Preview of Tragedy

An Unexpected Denial

Jeremiah's second recorded symbolic act requires him to turn his back on that which is so intrinsic to his Hebrew culture. He is divinely commanded not to marry and have children (Jer 16:1–4). Sadly, Jeremiah's line will cease to exist in ancient Israel. So unusual is celibacy in Hebrew society that no separate word for bachelor even exists in biblical Hebrew.[3] Furthermore, he is commanded not to mourn with those who mourn or rejoice with those who rejoice (16:5–9). This is hard. Such countercultural, antisocial behavior only exacerbates Jeremiah's already isolated and undesirable standing in the community. To the majority of Jerusalemites, this kind of behavior demonstrated beyond a reasonable doubt that Jeremiah was a false prophet and traitor, probably also mentally deranged.

A Severe Mercy

Is Yahweh so unfeeling that he would require this kind of personal sacrifice to proclaim his word? What at first sight seems hardhearted is in fact an act of severe mercy. Within a few years an unimaginable tragedy befalls Judah and Jerusalem. Because of the Judean government's rebellion against Babylon and the false hopes placed in Egypt, Nebuchadnezzar retaliates and unleashes total war against the little kingdom of Judah, reducing it to rubble. The loss of life is horrific. Tragically, in Topheth, the very place where Ahaz and Manasseh, kings of Judah, and other Judeans burned their sons and daughters in the fire (2 Kgs 16:3; 21:6; 23:10), a mass grave was hastily dug for rotting corpses as a consequence of the Babylonian siege.[4] There may not even have been time to

---

3. There is, however, a word in Modern Hebrew to express this concept (*ravvaq*), derived from a word meaning "empty."

4. Child sacrifice, an appalling atrocity, was practiced in order to demonstrate one's total devotion to a deity (usually a fertility god or goddess) and thereby secure special blessings, including other offspring, fruitful seasons,

45

cover the corpses, providing a grisly meal for scavenging animals and birds (Jer 7:33). In such appalling circumstances, there was no time to mourn the deceased. Yahweh precluded such a heartrending tragedy from befalling Jeremiah. There are times when a denial of pleasure turns out to be a blessing in disguise.

Jeremiah's antisocial behavior accompanies his constant preaching of doom and gloom. On occasion his listeners demand an explanation for his dire prophecies: "Why has the LORD decreed such a great disaster against us? What wrong have we done? What sin have we committed against the LORD our God?" (Jer 16:10). This of course provides Jeremiah with a teachable moment: an opportunity to drive home the necessity of heartfelt repentance and sincere reformation. Consequently, his withdrawal from ordinary society is an unspoken message to all whom he encounters. His antisocial behavior reinforces his verbal proclamation of the tragic consequences of covenant disloyalty.

Fellow Travelers

Jeremiah's celibacy is not a unique phenomenon in the Bible. In fact, we have a small number of great champions of the faith who were also celibate, including Elijah, Elisha, and John the Baptist, all three of whom were also prophets. It should be noted that, like Jeremiah, these men served in perilous times, John the Baptist even

---

and protection from one's enemies. Though explicitly forbidden in the Sinai covenant (Deut 12:31), apostate Judeans borrowed the practice from their pagan neighbors, especially the Ammonites, Moabites, and Phoenicians. Topheth is the name of a location in the valley of Ben Hinnom where this abomination was performed. The Hinnom Valley bounded the western hill of the Old City of Jerusalem and curved in a southeastwardly direction around to the Kidron Valley. Today, Jerusalem University College (formerly The American Institute of Holy Land Studies) sits along the line of the wall overlooking the Hinnom. Students at JUC can peer down into the valley below them and be reminded of the horrifying things that happened there. The place name for the valley was transliterated into Greek as Gehenna (from ge-hinnom in Hebrew), and it became a metaphor denoting the place of final punishment for the wicked. Jesus uses this term as a warning in his teaching on judgment (Matt 5:29–30; see NRSV marg.).

dying a martyr's death (Matt 14:1–2; Mark 6:14–29; Luke 9:7–9). Add to this list Jesus and Paul, who were both celibate and even spoke of circumstances in which celibacy would be a preferable option. According to Jesus, "The one who can accept this should accept it" (Matt 19:11–12). Paul personally prefers celibacy and urges those who have the gift of self-control to follow his example, on the grounds that singleness entails fewer restraints on ministry and frees one from anxieties over care for a spouse and children. But Paul recognizes that most believers will marry, and he gives his unqualified blessing to the state of matrimony (1 Cor 7:6–7, 25–40; Eph 5:22–33).

Extreme circumstances require extreme measures. This dictum certainly proved true for Jeremiah. The impending destruction of Jerusalem and the exile of Judah required extreme self-denial on Jeremiah's part. Though deprived the companionship of a loving wife and the joy of children, Yahweh mercifully spared him the anguish of witnessing their agonizing deaths and their being dumped into a mass grave. The thought of their corpses as carrion for scavengers would have haunted him to his dying day. Jeremiah is promised he will survive the ordeal; and he did survive, but without the tortured memories that accompany Holocaust survivors who lost their loved ones in the Nazi death camps. Jeremiah rightly belongs in the prophetic hall of fame. His obedience in the face of hardship and suffering is a triumph of commitment to God.[5]

Pots and Potsherds

Nothing is more commonly uncovered in archaeological excavations than pottery, especially fragments of pottery called potsherds. As it turns out, pottery is one of the most important diagnostic tools available to archaeologists for dating sites. The reason is that, like dishware and silverware today, certain styles and forms became the fashion at various times and thus function as crude

---

5. *New Analytical Bible*, 857.

timepieces. But for Jeremiah pottery serves as an effective means of mass communication. No other item he could have chosen was so durable, so ubiquitous, and so apt for a symbolic action.

The Potter and the Clay

Yahweh commands Jeremiah to go down to the house of a potter in Jerusalem (Jer 18).[6] While observing the potter at work, a word from Yahweh comes to Jeremiah. Much like his inaugural visions of the almond tree and the boiling pot (Jer 1:9–16), Jeremiah's observing something ordinary becomes an occasion for the extraordinary, a word from Yahweh. As we will see, this revelatory moment becomes the basis for another dramatic symbolic action.

But what did he see? As the potter was shaping a pot on a wheel, he was displeased with the result. He squeezed the clay into a new lump and reshaped it to his liking. The point of the action lies in the ability of the potter to completely remake the clay into a vessel that suits him. There is no mistaking who's who in this episode: Yahweh is the potter, and the house of Israel is the clay.

More importantly, what does it mean? It would be easy to read this passage solely in terms of the sovereignty of God. That is, God determines the eternal destiny of every human being. The immediate context, however, contains a clear note of contingency in the action of the potter upon the clay. Yahweh appeals to Israel (the clay) to repent and reform their ways. If they do so, he will reshape the destiny awaiting them. Thus, they can do something to alter the outcome. This note of contingency has been present all along in Jeremiah's messages.

---

6. The reference to "going down" accurately reflects the topography of the ancient City of David. The temple was located on the summit of Mt. Moriah. As one leaves the temple precincts and proceeds southward, the elevation rapidly drops until one arrives at the junction of the Kidron and Hinnom valleys. Potters and other craftsmen, whose work required copious amounts of water, lived near the lower pool and the En Rogel spring just outside the city walls at the southern end of the City of David.

Jeremiah's Symbolic Actions

Hurling a Pot

One of the most familiar English nursery rhymes is Humpty Dumpty:

> Humpty Dumpty sat on a wall,
> Humpty Dumpty had a great fall.
> All the king's horses and all the king's men
> Couldn't put Humpty together again.

This little ditty aptly captures Jeremiah's symbolic action with the pot. He pulls off a show-and-tell with dramatic effect. Here are the sequential stages of this symbolic act:

- He buys an earthenware jar. We're probably talking about a water jug or flask of some size.
- He gathers a few elders and senior priests and leads them out the Potsherd Gate to the Hinnom Valley.
- He proceeds to deliver a hard-hitting message announcing the imminent destruction of Jerusalem and the theological reason for it.
- He pours water from the jar, symbolizing the end of Judah.[7]
- He then breaks the jar in their presence.
- He adds a final word of explanation, though none was needed. You can be sure they got the point.

Several aspects of this effective sign-act require further comment. Although the text doesn't explicitly say so, I suspect Jeremiah hurled the jar from the top of a cliff overlooking the Hinnom Valley, where it shattered into smithereens. The selection of the Hinnom was apropos and convenient since it lay just outside the Potsherd Gate of Jerusalem in Jeremiah's day. This portion of the

---

7. Admittedly, the English text doesn't explicitly say this, but we probably have a wordplay between "jug" (*baqbuq*) and "make void" (*baqaq*). The word *baqbuq* is an onomatopoeic word resembling the sound of liquid being poured out of a jar or jug. The action and accompanying sound underscore Jeremiah's words.

Hinnom Valley is bounded by rocky cliffs—a perfect launch pad for Jeremiah's jar. In effect, Jeremiah becomes a pot-putter![8]

But Jeremiah selected the Hinnom Valley for more than mere convenience. This was also the location of Topheth, an altar used to offer children to Baal and Molech (Jer 19:4–5; cf. 7:30–32; 2 Kgs 23:10). This abomination, borrowed from the Canaanites, was practiced by some of the kings of Judah as well as ordinary citizens. In keeping with the principle of *lex talionis* (the punishment must fit the crime), in the very place where the skeletons of children were buried after being burned on the altar, the corpses of Jerusalemites and Judeans would be buried in a mass grave in connection with the Babylonian siege of 588–586 BC. The horror of what happened there would be stigmatized by a new name, the Valley of Slaughter. As previously mentioned, this horrible place became a terrifying symbol of final punishment in the NT.

As it turns out, another tragic event took place in this vicinity. Judas Iscariot, who betrayed Jesus, committed suicide nearby. In fact, a plot of land on the southern slopes of Hinnom is named Akeldama (field of blood) to commemorate the purchase of this property by either Judas or the high priests (Matt 27:3–10; Acts 1:16–20). What is significant for our study is that Matthew links Jeremiah 18–19 to what happened to Judas.[9] Truly a somber place.

Wearing a Yoke

We come now to Jeremiah's most dramatic and effective symbolic act. For this performance, I award Jeremiah runner-up in the category of Oscar for Best Symbolic Action. Not only was it theatrical, it was downright disturbing—so much so that it drew the ire of a prophet named Hananiah, who performed a counter symbolic action.

---

8. This is a lame attempt to make a pun by inventing a new word. As most readers know, there is an event from track and field in which an athlete hurls a sixteen-pound iron ball for distance, called the shot put. One who competes in this event is called a shot-putter. I wonder how far Jeremiah put his pot!

9. This creative reinterpretation of an OT text links together Zech 11:12–13 and Jer 18–19.

JEREMIAH'S SYMBOLIC ACTIONS

This bizarre symbolic act is initiated by the word of Yahweh near the beginning of Zedekiah's reign (ca. 597 BC). As it turns out, he will be the last king of Judah. Only ten years remain until Judah is devastated, the city and temple destroyed, and the state demoted to a small province within the mighty Babylonian Empire. Here is how Jeremiah's symbolic action unfolds:

- Jeremiah makes for himself a yoke of straps and bars. This is a piece of equipment ordinarily used to harness and control animals such as oxen or donkeys to pull a plow. Unexpectedly and dramatically, Jeremiah wears the yoke around his neck as he goes about the city. That it quickly draws attention—and becomes a public nuisance—hardly needs mentioning, nor is its meaning difficult to discern. The yoke and straps speak of submission to authority, namely, Nebuchadnezzar king of Babylon.

- Jeremiah's initial audience is not the crowds at the temple or in the city but envoys from the neighboring countries of Edom, Moab, Ammon, Tyre, and Sidon. They were meeting with Zedekiah's cabinet and mapping out a coordinated strategy to rebel against King Nebuchadnezzar of Babylon. Jeremiah's symbolic action signifies the futility of the attempt. This ill-advised rebellion was probably sparked by two events: a revolt in the Babylonian army (December 595–January 594 BC) and the accession of a new and aggressive Egyptian pharaoh, Psammeticus II. Judah, occupying the land bridge between Asia and Africa, sought an opportunity to recover their independence by allying themselves with Egypt.[10] Jeremiah warns the envoys not to be deceived: the God of Israel has handed their kingdoms over to King Nebuchadnezzar and his successors until the third generation (Jer 27:7). Like a docile work animal, they should accept the burden of submitting to the divinely enabled mastery of Nebuchadnezzar. To

---

10. Illustrating once again the old adage "politics makes strange bedfellows." In 609 BC, Pharaoh Neco II snuffed out the aspirations of King Josiah and a resurgent Judah. Now, some fifteen years later, Egypt is viewed as an ally and savior.

51

resist entails terrible punishment by sword, famine, and pestilence (Jer 27:8). By no means should these leaders harken to their misguided prophets, diviners, dreamers, soothsayers, and sorcerers who claim, "You will not serve the king of Babylon" (Jer 27:9). Jeremiah instructs the envoys to convey his message to their respective kings.

- Jeremiah then speaks personally to Zedekiah and warns him against the folly of listening to the lies of the Judean false prophets and joining the rebellion (Jer 27:12). Jeremiah bluntly tells Zedekiah that Yahweh has not sent them.

- Jeremiah finally appeals to the priests and people. This no doubt takes place once again within the temple precincts. He warns them against the empty prophesying of the false prophets. He dramatically concludes with a prophecy of his own. If the nation persists in rebellion, the remaining sacred objects, the bronze pillars, the large water basin, and the rest of the temple vessels will be transported to Babylon and added to the temple objects already removed in the days of King Jeconiah (Jehoiachin). We should note, however, that Jeremiah inserts a small glimmer of hope right at the end. The temple objects will not remain indefinitely in the land of Babylon; a day is coming when they will be returned to the temple mount (Jer 27:22). In case you're wondering, Jeremiah was right on. In the book of Ezra, we learn that these items were indeed returned and placed in the Second Temple (Ezra 1:7–11).

- Hananiah, a false prophet from Gibeon, confronts Jeremiah with a counter symbolic action (Jer 28). What unfolds is one of the more dramatic confrontations in the Old Testament. We will investigate this in more detail in the next chapter but for now simply summarize what happened. Hananiah, enraged at Jeremiah's symbolic action, decides to humiliate and silence him. He comes up to Jeremiah and forcibly takes the yoke off Jeremiah's neck and utters his own prophecy. In short, he makes a bold counterclaim that the yoke of

Babylonian oppression will be broken and Judah will experience freedom. We will return to this episode later and narrate "the rest of the story" when we take up the whole issue of false prophets in chapter 4.

Buying a Field

Finally, we consider Jeremiah's only symbolic action conveying hope—which, ironically, comes not during a time of hope but during a time of despair.

Setting and Sequence

Two settings for chapter 32 need to be distinguished. Historically, the symbolic action unfolds shortly before the destruction of Jerusalem (ca. 587–586 BC). The city was undergoing a horrific siege, with enormous loss of life from "sword, famine, and pestilence" just as Jeremiah had warned. The prophet was "confined in the courtyard of the guard in the royal palace of Judah" (Jer 32:2). The literary setting for this symbolic action must also be taken into account. Chapter 32 is part of a cohesive unit, chapters 30–33, often styled "the Book of Consolation," in which (predominantly) poetic oracles and a lengthy prose narrative paint a rosy future for a renewed and restored people of God under a new covenant. In the end Yahweh will fulfill his promised redemption of the whole house of Israel and Judah (Jer 33:14, 24–26). This section thus counterbalances the preponderance of judgment oracles in the book of Jeremiah. I leave to the last chapter the task of unpacking the details of this eschatological transformation.

The symbolic action unfolds in the following sequence:

- Yahweh reveals to Jeremiah that his cousin Hanamel wishes to sell a field in Anathoth. Hanamel was probably reduced to poverty as a result of the Babylonian invasion and desperately needed the money to survive.[11] Jeremiah, being the nearest male relative, had first right to acquire the land, according to the property law of Lev 25:25–28. The unspoken question is, Why would Jeremiah actually make such a foolhardy purchase?

- As revealed, Hanamel seeks out the incarcerated Jeremiah and makes the offer. Jeremiah realizes this is from Yahweh.

- Jeremiah follows the legal procedures to acquire the right to the property. It should be noted that according to the theology of Mt. Sinai, individuals don't actually "own" property; they lease the land from Yahweh, the rightful owner, and thereby benefit from its produce. When, however, an "owner" transfers "ownership" of landed property, this transaction is validated by an original bill of sale and a copy, both signed by the buyer and witnessed by several witnesses. According to our text, this is precisely what Jeremiah did. The asking price is a mere seventeen pieces of silver, reflecting the depressed economy brought on by the Babylonian invasion. In this instance, both the original deed, which is folded and sealed, and the copy, which is left open, are stored in a clay jar for safekeeping and entrusted to Baruch.[12]

- A further word reveals that this sale conveys an important theological truth: a day is coming when once again the land will be productive and available for sale. In short, a time of prosperity would return to the now devastated countryside. Beyond the present judgment lies future blessing.

---

11. "The Babylonian army was perhaps already encamped at Anathoth, which lay only three miles north of Jerusalem." Lundbom, *Prophet Like Moses*, 158.

12. The type of jar used was probably similar to those found at Qumran in which the famous Dead Sea Scrolls were stored.

Jeremiah's Symbolic Actions

Significance

Jeremiah's purchase is followed by his prayer and a promise from Yahweh. His prayer recaps the essential elements of the Sinai covenant and recites Israel's abject failure to keep covenant. Important to note is the keynote affirmation at the beginning of the prayer: "Nothing is too hard for you" (Jer 32:17). One hears echoes of God's response to Abraham and Sarah's question about an heir: "Is anything too hard for the LORD?" (Gen 18:14). The divine word that comes to Jeremiah appropriately picks up on this query: "Is anything too hard for me?" (Jer 32:27). The answer, of course, is no. The kingdom of God will overcome all obstacles and opponents. The exile of Judah will certainly be followed by a return to the land. And the return to the land will be followed by a time of unparalleled blessing. The NT unpacks the thrilling conclusion to the biblical history of redemption. The point is this: no matter how dark and despairing things may appear at a given point in the story of redemption, as they did in the days of Jeremiah, the ultimate outcome is glorious beyond words. In the words of the hymn, "Jesus shall reign where'er the sun / does its successive journey run, / his kingdom stretch from shore to shore, / till moon shall wax and wane no more" (Isaac Watts). In the meantime, the Lord's Prayer is the believer's hope and stay: "Your kingdom come, your will be done, on earth as it is in heaven" (Matt 6:10). And so it shall.

SYMBOLIC ACTS IN THE NEW TESTAMENT

As the long-expected prophet like Moses (Deut 18:15–19; cf. John 1:21; Acts 3:17–26; 7:37–38) who speaks God's final word (Heb 1:1–2), Jesus also performed symbolic acts. No gospel emphasizes this more than the Gospel of John, which is structured around a series of symbolic actions. The gospel falls neatly into two main sections: a "Book of Signs" (1:19—12:50) and a "Book of Glory" (13:1—20:31). The former consists of seven signs that point to Jesus as the divine Son who is the Word of God in flesh. Of these seven signs, five are clearly sign-acts. Thus, the first sign, changing water to wine (John 2:1–11), demonstrates the superiority of Jesus's new message to the old teaching of Judaism. The feeding of the five thousand proclaims Jesus as the Bread of Life, the one who is superior to the heavenly manna of the wilderness generation (John 6:1–15, 25–59). A third symbolic action involves Jesus walking on the Sea of Galilee during a storm. This powerfully portrays Jesus as the Lord of nature and links him with passages in the Psalms in which Yahweh controls the forces of nature, especially unruly forces like the raging sea (e.g., Pss 33:7: 65:7; 77:19). A fourth symbolic act, the miracle of the healing of a blind man at the Pool of Siloam (John 9:1–41), dramatically illuminates Jesus as the Light of the world. In an extraordinary fifth symbolic act, Jesus raises Lazarus from the dead and thereby demonstrates that he himself embodies the resurrection and life everlasting (John 11:1–44). But in effect, the Book of Glory culminates in what could properly be called a climactic eighth sign, the resurrection of Jesus. In Jewish numerology, eight represents a new beginning; Jesus's resurrection fittingly ushers in a new beginning, the long-expected Age to Come. From a literary perspective, the resurrection of Jesus functions as a counterpoint to the prologue. That is, not only does Jesus, as the Word of God, create the world but, as the Son of God, he also creates a new world by means of his death and resurrection. There were no doubt other symbolic actions performed by Jesus during his earthly ministry (John 21:25). But the greatest of these is his resurrection; as the Apostle Paul affirms, Christian faith stands or falls on its veracity (1 Cor 15:12–19).

The Synoptic Gospels (Matthew, Mark, and Luke) add their witness to the symbolic acts recorded in John's Gospel. For example, Matthew and Mark record Jesus's curse on a barren fig tree during Passion Week (Matt 21:18–22; Mark 11:12–25). Most scholars agree that this event was a symbolic act in that the fig tree was a well-known symbol for the nation of Israel. Rather than being an instance of personal annoyance, the curse foretold the fate of Jerusalem in the years following Jesus's death and resurrection—fulfilled in the destruction of the city and temple by the Romans in AD 70.

Most likely Jesus's cleansing of the temple functioned as another symbolic action, an event recorded by all the Gospels (Mark 11:15–19; Matt 21:12–13, 18–22; Luke 19:45–48; John 2:13–22). In this confrontational episode, one hears echoes of the prophet Jeremiah's temple sermon. Indeed, one can't help remembering Jeremiah's courageous denunciation in that the Synoptic evangelists all attribute to Jesus a direct quote from Jeremiah's famous sermon: "Is it not written, 'My house shall be called a house of prayer for all the nations'? But you have made it 'a den of robbers'" (Mark 11:17; Matt 21:13; Luke 19:46; cf. Jer 7:11 and Isa 56:7). This is perhaps another reason why many of Jesus's contemporaries thought he was the prophet Jeremiah come back from the dead (Matt 16:14).[13]

In terms of magnitude and scope, of course, none of the symbolic actions performed by the Old Testament prophets even remotely compare with those of Jesus. He is without peer in this regard. This is especially the case in Jesus's most meaningful symbolic action, narrated by all three Synoptics but curiously omitted by John: the Last Supper.[14] This simple meal—consisting of but two elements, bread and wine, representing Jesus's body and blood given on behalf of sinners—lies at the center of Christian experience and worship. Without doubt this symbolic action has captured the hearts and minds of more human beings than any ever performed. Without any intent to be flippant, I unhesitatingly award to Jesus the Oscar for Best Symbolic Action Ever. And who among the redeemed would disagree?

---

13. Especially so if, in fact, there was a cleansing of the temple at the beginning of Jesus's ministry as narrated in John's Gospel.

14. Note, however, that John's Upper Room discourse is clearly placed in a Passover context. The discourse on the Bread of Life gives the essence of what is embodied in the Last Supper (John 6).

4

Jeremiah and the False Prophets

INTRODUCTION

One of the most difficult aspects of Jeremiah's ministry, particularly after King Josiah passed from the scene, involved bitter opposition by individuals who claimed to be prophets of Yahweh. These so-called prophets mocked and reviled Jeremiah. Unfortunately, they were in the majority and Jeremiah seemed a lonely dissenting voice, out of sync and out of touch. These prophets, whom Jeremiah doesn't hesitate to call "false prophets," emphasized patriotic nationalism and downplayed the ethical and moral demands of the Sinai covenant. In their view, routine ritualism was the remedy for national survival. Over against this, Jeremiah pleaded for genuine repentance and a return to the moral standards of the Sinai covenant.[1] Unsurprisingly, the false prophets garnered the support of Judean civil and religious leaders

---

1. Jeremiah and the other genuine prophets were not opposed to the cultic activity of the priesthood per se (see Jer 6:20; 7:21–23; 14:11; Hos 8:13; 9:4; Isa 1:11–17; Mic 6:7–8). Rather, they opposed a mechanical, magical view of the cult, such that mere performance secured divine blessing and success. In fact, Jeremiah envisioned a resumption of the cult in the restoration (Jer 33:18).

JEREMIAH AND THE FALSE PROPHETS

and a majority of citizens. It was, after all, much easier "to go with the flow." As a consequence, Jeremiah endured abuse and ostracism from his countrymen. Since only a small minority took him seriously, he was forced to watch a national catastrophe unfold like a slow motion replay of a train wreck. As we saw earlier, his courageous preaching resulted in vilification and persecution as a traitor, in the course of which he was mobbed by an angry crowd (Jer 26); beaten by government officials (Jer 37:15); thrown into an empty cistern, where he nearly died of dehydration (Jer 37:16; 38:5–13); and incarcerated in the court of the guard (Jer 37:21; 38:13). Ironically, it was an Ethiopian court official, Ebed-melech (Jer 38:7–13), and Nebuchadnezzar, king of the Babylonians, who spared Jeremiah's life from his fellow countrymen (Jer 39:11–14). The conflict between Jeremiah and the false prophets of his day raises a number of important theological issues relevant for our own. This becomes the focus of the present chapter.

QUALIFICATIONS OF A TRUE PROPHET

An examination of false prophecy must begin with an understanding of the qualifications for the office of prophet.[2] First of all, being a prophet was not dependent upon one's ancestry. In contrast to monarch or priest, in Hebrew society, the office of prophet was egalitarian.[3] This is confirmed by a survey of the background of individuals recognized by Hebrew tradition as genuine prophets. The fellowship of the prophets reflects a cross-section of Hebrew society, ranging from aristocratic to rustic (Isaiah and Amos). Furthermore, the office was not elective. True prophets did not run for the office, nor were they elected by a democratic or oligarchic

---

2. For further discussion, see Helyer, *Yesterday*, 254–57.

3. In order to be a king of Israel or Judah, one must be a male descendant of the royal family. In the north (Israel) there were several different royal dynasties; in the south, with but one exception, namely the usurper Queen Athaliah, all monarchs were descendants of King David of the tribe of Judah and house of Jesse. The priesthood was similarly restricted to a particular family, namely, the male descendants of the family of Aaron from the tribe of Levi. Only Levites could serve as ministers in the tabernacle or temple.

process. In fact, many genuine prophets tried to run from it—Moses, Isaiah, Jeremiah, Amos, and especially Jonah. It was a daunting task. Furthermore, the office of prophet, though typically male, was not confined to men. There were three outstanding women who distinguished themselves as true prophets of Yahweh: Deborah, Huldah, and Noadiah. Almost certainly there were other unnamed women who faithfully served as prophets (see, e.g., Isa 8:3). It should be noted that in the NT Anna was a prophet (Luke 2:36) and the gift of prophecy was not confined to men (Acts 1:17–18, quoting Joel 2:28–29; 1 Cor 11:5).

That brings us to the one indispensable requirement for serving as a mouthpiece of Yahweh. One must be called by Yahweh himself in order to stand in his council and speak in his name. The Hebrew Scriptures emphasize this indispensable qualification setting a prophet apart from his or her peers. The book of Jeremiah serves as a primary witness to this nonnegotiable prerequisite.

JEREMIAH'S INDICTMENT OF THE FALSE PROPHETS

Jeremiah's defense of his own authority as a prophet and his corresponding indictment of the false prophets is a major contribution to the theology of the OT and its relevance for understanding the theology of the NT. Chapters 23 and 26–29 bring us to the heart of the matter. We begin, however, with a passage in 4:9–10 that sets up the problem. In this text Jeremiah laments the fact that the people of Judah and Jerusalem have been deceived by prophetic oracles that assure them of safety when in fact a sword is at their throats. How can this be? How can Yahweh allow such a situation? This state of affairs tortures Jeremiah throughout his ministry. A partial answer unfolds in chapter 23. It falls into three sections:

- Oracle condemning the civil leaders of Israel, called "shepherds" (vv. 1–4).
- Salvation oracle promising a just and righteous king from the line of David, styled "a righteous Branch" (vv. 5–8).

Jeremiah and the False Prophets

- Series of oracles denouncing the false prophets (vv. 9–40). Our interest centers on this third section.

Jeremiah's indictment unfolds in the following manner:
- Topic sentence introducing the oracles against the false prophets (v. 9a).
- First lament: the deplorable spiritual condition of the false prophets (vv. 9b–11). Jeremiah recounts his personal reaction to the false prophets. Their behavior and preaching affect him emotionally, physically, and spiritually. The glaring disconnect between what they should be and what they are profoundly disturbs him.
- First judgment oracle (introduced by "Therefore"): The false prophets are accomplices in the imminent national catastrophe (v. 12). The striking imagery of falling off a slippery and dark trail graphically describes their self-chosen path and its tragic consequences.
- Second lament: the guilt of the Judean false prophets (vv. 13–14). Worth noting is the comparison between the false prophets of Samaria (shorthand for the northern kingdom of Israel) who prophesied in the name of the false god Baal ("this repulsive thing") and the "more shocking thing" (NRSV) committed by the prophets in Judah. The latter learned nothing from the disaster that befell the north. Instead, they plunged into adultery (both spiritual and physical) and encouraged wickedness by their hypocrisy. Jeremiah likens them to the notorious people of Sodom and Gomorrah in the days of Abraham (Gen 18–19).
- Second judgment oracle ("Therefore"): This oracle is couched in the first person. Yahweh himself speaks and decrees punishment for the false prophets. "Wormwood and poisoned water" (NRSV) refers to a bitter herb and contaminated water, both of which can be life-threatening. Their punishment is just because they actually encouraged ungodliness in the land (v. 15).

- Divine oracle of warning and indictment (vv. 16–17): This passage brings us to the heart of Jeremiah's charge against the false prophets. Their false messages of hope spring from their own stubborn hearts and not the heart of God. In short, they were neither summoned nor commissioned by Yahweh. They failed to meet the one indispensable requirement for being a mouthpiece of Yahweh, namely, a divine call.

- Third judgment oracle (vv. 19–20): Jeremiah depicts divine judgment metaphorically as a violent storm, an oft-observed weather phenomenon during the Palestinian rainy season (October through April). According to Jeremiah, the inflicted judgment will be both severe and certain. The oracle ends, however, with an intriguing comment: "In the latter days you will understand clearly" (v. 20 NRSV). Presumably, this refers to the days of renewal and restoration lying in an unspecified future. I will say more about this in the next chapter.

- The chapter concludes with a lengthy section quite remarkable for its point of view (vv. 21–40). The passage is once again couched in the first person and the voice speaking is none other than Yahweh himself. I call attention to this phenomenon, a hallmark of genuine prophecy, because it occurs frequently in Jeremiah—indeed, in all the canonical prophets. The prophet recedes into the background and speaks as the very mouthpiece of God himself. The problem is that a false prophet may imitate this mode as well, which raises to an acute level a question occupying our attention in the rest of this chapter. How can one tell when a true prophet of God is speaking?

THE TESTS FOR A TRUE PROPHET

The Hebrew Scriptures provide the people of God with some tests for distinguishing true and false prophets.[4] Knowing full well the tendencies of the human heart to turn away from revealed truth

4. See Helyer, *Yesterday*, 277–83.

(Jer 17:9–10), specific guidance is essential for determining who really speaks for Yahweh. The book of Deuteronomy provides two tests whereby the faithful may discern false prophets. These two tests may be categorized as follows:

- The empirical test (Deut 18): This test assumes that what Yahweh promises he will accomplish. This of course is a corollary to the doctrine of God's sovereignty. The test itself, however, is a negative test; it only excludes from consideration. For example, the status of a person claiming to be a prophet but not making a specific prophecy is uncertain. If, however, a self-proclaimed prophet does predict such and so and it fails to come to pass, then one may confidently conclude that Yahweh did not speak that word.

- The theological test (Deut 13): But what if a prophet seems to pass the empirical test? Does that automatically mean such a person is a true prophet of Yahweh? Deuteronomy 13 depicts a situation in which "a prophet or one who foretells by dreams" (v. 1) appears and promises omens or portents. Furthermore, the promised omens or portents take place as announced. Should it be assumed, then, in light of the empirical test, that this must surely be the word of Yahweh? The theological test functions as a crucial caveat. If, despite fulfillment, such individuals suggest or urge that other gods be acknowledged and followed, the verdict is clear: they are false prophets. In short, only the one, true and living God is to be acknowledged and obeyed. His revealed will constitutes the touchstone for faith and practice. To suggest or encourage a departure from this standard is treason against Yahweh and merits capital punishment (v. 5). Note carefully how the empirical test must be used in tandem with the theological test. To ignore one or the other may allow a false prophet to slip through the grid.

With these two tests in hand, we return to the classic confrontation between Jeremiah and Hananiah (Jer 27–28). The setting is about 594–593 BC. Yahweh summons Jeremiah to perform a symbolic act in which he wears a yoke on his neck. The message to neighboring envoys, the civil and religious leadership of Judah, and the people of Jerusalem and Judah is clear: Nebuchadnezzar of Babylon will impose his rule on the peoples of the great land bridge between Mesopotamia and Egypt. I surmise Jeremiah wore his yoke regularly in his movements about Jerusalem and in the temple precincts as a constant reminder of impending disaster. This disheartening and frightening message so infuriated a prophet by the name of Hananiah that he accosted Jeremiah. This dramatic confrontation, as with many of Jeremiah's most memorable moments, took place in the house of Yahweh, doubtless during a festival or specially convened assembly.

Not content with mere refutation, Hananiah counters with a symbolic action of his own. He humiliates Jeremiah by jerking the yoke off his neck and breaking it before all the onlookers. You can be sure this was not done gently! Hananiah then dramatically announces a prediction in the name of Yahweh. He will remove Nebuchadnezzar's control over all the nations in the region and do so within two years. One can easily imagine the effect upon the audience. No doubt a groundswell of rejoicing and thanksgiving resounded in the temple courtyard. After all, the people desperately hoped to hear this, a word of deliverance.

What did Jeremiah do? He said nothing and left the scene. Seemingly, Hananiah had thoroughly discredited him and gained the support of the vast majority of those present. Had an opinion poll been taken, it would have registered overwhelming support for Hananiah as a true prophet and denounced Jeremiah as a pretender and traitor. But now, "the rest of the story."[5]

Because Hananiah accompanied his prophecy of deliverance with a prediction, this brings into play the empirical test. The problem, of course, entails the two-year interval before one can confirm or refute its truthfulness. What do the people of God do during the interim? Does the theological test (Deut 13) resolve the issue? Unfortunately, there is no immediate answer because there

---

5. To quote a well-known tagline used by former radio personality Paul Harvey.

is no indication in the text that Hananiah ever spoke in the name of a false god or suggested the people follow another god. The only option available seems to be "wait and see." In reality, however, they've already made up their minds: Hananiah must be the true prophet because he offers hope. Seemingly, nothing Jeremiah could do or say would change their minds.

Sometime later, however, Jeremiah responds to Hananiah's counter-symbolic action. According to the word of Yahweh, says Jeremiah, the wooden yoke Hananiah easily broke will be replaced with one he can't, a yoke of iron. Yahweh has decreed Nebuchadnezzar's complete subjugation of the surrounding peoples, Judah included. The text does not indicate if this rejoinder was public or private. I assume it was public.

Then Jeremiah cuts to the heart of the matter. The fundamental problem lies in Hananiah's presuming to speak in the name of Yahweh. In fact, he has not been commissioned despite his apparent acceptance by the overwhelming majority. Then Jeremiah ups the ante. The people will not have to wait two years for confirmation of Hananiah's prediction. Within a year, says Jeremiah, Hananiah will die. This stunning prediction at least narrows the time frame for the empirical test to come into play. The text laconically informs the reader that Hananiah died in the seventh month (v. 17). According to Jeremiah 28:1, the initial confrontation took place in the fifth month (August/September) and Hananiah's death occurred in the seventh month (November/December). Jeremiah's rebuttal dramatically shortens the time frame for the empirical test to be applied. It must be admitted, however, that there was a period of uncertainty, in this case two months. Given that there is no indication in the text that Hananiah urged the people to follow another god or transgress the law of Moses, we are left with some short-term ambiguity. Whether anyone was persuaded by Hananiah's death is not stated. I suspect it changed very few opinions. At least Hananiah was spared the embarrassment of having to explain the nonfulfillment of his bold prediction!

As already stated, Jeremiah's indictment goes well beyond Hananiah's reckless prediction. He is also guilty of speaking rebellion against Yahweh because Yahweh didn't commission him as a prophet (v. 16). This is the bottom line in Jeremiah's conflict with his opponents who claimed to be true prophets. None of them truly stood in the council of Yahweh (Jer 23:21-22). They were frauds who prophesied out of "the delusions of their own minds" (14:14).

Is there anything else that might have enabled a verdict at the time of the contradictory prophecies? As it turns out, a third test does assist in resolving the ambiguity. Briefly stated, this test requires that a true prophet who stands in the council of Yahweh must also walk in the ways of Yahweh as spelled out in the Sinai covenant. We may label this the ethical and moral test. In short, the true prophet must "walk the talk." We return to the central passage in Jeremiah 23. Here it becomes evident that an important—indeed, crucial—aspect of being a spokesperson for Yahweh involves a life that corresponds to the requirements of the Sinai covenant. What crushed Jeremiah's spirit was the wholesale disregard for the covenant stipulations. The notion that one could presume to speak in the name of Yahweh all the while flouting his will was utter folly. Note how Jeremiah characterizes the prophets of his day:

- They are adulterers, unfaithful to both Yahweh and their wives (23:10, 14).
- Their behavior is evil (23:10).
- They abuse their power (23:10).
- They resemble the notorious inhabitants of Sodom and Gomorrah (23:11, 14).
- They actually strengthen the hands of evildoers instead of calling upon them to repent (23:14, 22).
- They lie about the source of their optimistic prophecies.
- The source of their prophecy is falsehood and empty imaginations (23:21-32).

With biting irony, Jeremiah employs a play on words. The Hebrew word *massa'* has the basic meaning of "burden or heavy load." But it may also have a transferred meaning of "oracle."[6] Thus the false prophets claim to deliver a word of Yahweh, but in reality they only convey a heavy load to carry. To round out this vivid wordplay, Jeremiah, speaking as Yahweh's personal spokesperson, says, "I will surely *lift you up and cast you away* from my presence, you and the city" (23:39; italics mine). What makes this wordplay effective is that the verbal noun *mass'a* refers to the act of lifting or removing a heavy load. The bottom line in the condemnation of the false prophets lies in this tragic epithet: "everlasting disgrace—everlasting shame that will not be forgotten" (23:40).

Nonetheless, it must be admitted that for a short while, in this case two months, no definitive test lay at hand to declare immediately and indisputably who spoke in the name of Yahweh. It's worth remembering, however, that Jeremiah is not the only one who still maintains covenant faithfulness. As always, there is a remnant who remain steadfast (cf. 1 Kgs 19:18). One may be quite sure that among these servants of Yahweh there was little or no confusion. They knew in their hearts that Jeremiah truly spoke the word of Yahweh. An inner certainty whose source lay in the Spirit of God guided them in discerning the truth.

THE NT AND FALSE PROPHECY

The NT offers abundant evidence that false prophecy continued to be a problem in the new-covenant era. Jesus warned his disciples: "Watch out for false prophets. They come to you in sheep's clothing, but inwardly they are ferocious wolves" (Matt 7:15); "For false messiahs and false prophets will appear and perform signs and omens, to deceive, if possible, even the elect. So be on your guard; I have told you everything ahead of time" (Mark 13:22–23). The NT epistles bear out Jesus's warning. Paul, Peter, and John address this recurring threat to the spiritual life of the emerging church (2 Cor 11:13; 2 Tim 3:1–9; 2 Pet 2:1; 1 John 4:1; Rev 2:14–16, 20–25).

---

6. Or, alternatively, there may be a Hebrew homonym meaning "a pronouncement or utterance."

What is interesting and relevant for our discussion is whether we find similar tests for false prophets in NT literature. The short answer is yes. Embedded in the teaching of Jesus and apostolic pastoral letters are the equivalents of the three tests for false prophets found in the OT.

The Empirical Test

Jesus warned his disciples that false prophets would arise and make astounding claims: "If anyone says to you, 'Look, here is the Messiah!' or, 'Look! there he is!' do not believe it" (Mark 13:21). None of the prophetic oracles proclaiming the coming of the Messiah leading up to the Jewish War of AD 66–70 turned out to be true. They were all false hopes. As it turns out, this was merely the first wave of failed messianic hopes. Jewish history from the first century AD to present times is littered with outbursts of fervent messianism.[7] The most recent failed messianic claim stemming from Jewish circles of which I am aware involved the late Rebbe Menachem Mendel Schneersohn, leader of the Chabad-Lubavitch Hasidic community in Brooklyn, New York. His followers enthusiastically proclaimed that he was the Messiah. I remember seeing posters in Jerusalem making this claim. For his part, he never affirmed the assertion, but neither did he categorically deny it. The hopes of the community were dashed, however, when Schneerson died on June 12, 1994. Nonetheless, some adherents continue to believe he will appear as the Messiah and usher in the messianic age, though their numbers dwindle with each passing year.[8]

---

7. In AD 132 a second Jewish revolt against Rome erupted in the land of Israel led by a man named Bar Cosiba. The flames of messianism were fueled by Rabbi Akiva, who renamed the rebel leader Bar Kochba, meaning "son of the star." This alludes to Num 24:17, a text already understood as messianic by Jewish interpreters. Of the many pretenders to be the Jewish messiah, none gained more notoriety than Shabbatai Zevi in the seventeenth century. For details, see Green, "False Messiahs," 2:883.

8. According to Green, "Under the leadership of the most recent Lubavitcher Rebbe, Menachem Mendel Schneersohn, this messianic fervor reached its most fevered pitch" (Green, "False Messiahs," 887). Among Hasidic

Messianic predictions have by no means been confined to Jewish circles. In fact, Christians have frequently climbed aboard the messianic bandwagon and gone out on a limb by predicting the return of Christ. The number of such episodes is past reckoning. Suffice to say, they all have been mistaken and thereby failed the empirical test. Jesus's words should be taken seriously: "But about that day or hour no one knows, neither the angels in heaven, nor the Son, but only the Father" (Mark 13:32).[9]

Worth noting are some comments in 2 Peter about false prophets. In this case, false prophets were actually employing the empirical test against apostolic teaching. That is, the false prophets reinterpreted the prophecies about the second coming of Christ because of their nonfulfillment. The late apostolic and post-apostolic leaders were thus put on the defensive. Their rejoinder amounted to this: Neither Jesus nor any of the apostles actually set a date for Jesus's return. To be sure, they expected that it would happen in their lifetime, but they did not teach that it would.[10] Second Peter reminds Christian readers that God isn't bound by human notions of time and will certainly fulfill his word at the appointed time. As certainly as God created the present world by a mere word of his mouth, so too will he, on the day of the Lord, create a new heaven and new earth by his all-powerful word (2 Pet 3:5, 13). Meanwhile, the watchword is to wait in hope and patience, recognizing that he delays in order to show mercy to many (2 Pet 3:9).

Jews generally, the expectation exists that the Messiah is potentially present in every age. The preventing factor is the religious failure of Jews to live according to Torah. Thus the urgency of the Chabad community to appeal to all Jews to repent and conform to Torah observance, to become a *ba'al teshuvah* ("a repentant"). The Hebrew word to describe observant Jews is *dati*, meaning "knowing" (i.e., knowing how to live one's life properly before God).

9. Alas, the notoriety and profitability of publishing supposed dates for Jesus's return virtually guarantees that there will be no end to such prognosticators.

10. In this regard it is instructive how the Apostle Paul's perspective on the timing of Jesus's return changed over time. In his earlier letters he expects that he will be alive when Christ returns. It became clear, however, as Paul neared the end of this life, that he would not live to see it.

The Theological Test

A number of clear examples of this test appear in NT pastoral letters. Throughout his church-planting trips, Paul encountered determined and disruptive counter missions. Paul's most persistent opponents were the so-called Judaizers. They were primarily Jews, but also included a few Gentiles convinced by the Judaizing agenda. Professing faith in Jesus as the Messiah, they adamantly insisted that membership in the new covenant people of God required observance of some of the distinctive practices of Judaism. To be specific, this entailed circumcision for men and strict observance of Sabbath and Kashrut (Jewish dietary regulations). Paul reacted strenuously against this imposition of Jewish "works" on the gospel of freedom and grace in Christ (Rom 3:19–31; 7:4–6; 2 Cor 3:7–18). Several Pauline letters exhibit his anger against those who advocated this deviation (Gal 5:3–4, 12; 2 Cor 11:13–15; Phil 3:2; Col 2:16).

The Apostle John likewise confronted doctrinal deviation from apostolic teaching. A close reading of his letters reveals that a different kind of false teaching began to appear near the end of the first Christian century. There is near unanimity that the doctrinal aberration was an early form of Gnosticism. This philosophical-theological system was predicated on a fundamental dualism between matter and spirit in which the former was inferior and evil and the latter was superior and good. The aim of salvation in such a scheme is to escape or be rescued from the clutches of matter, that is, the flesh (body) and the entire world system in which created beings live. The Christian version of Gnosticism offered Christ as a pure Spirit who reveals to the enlightened the true state of their existence. Once the illuminated receive this "knowledge" (*gnosis* in Greek), they are enabled by secret rituals and formulae to escape the prison house of the body and ascend into the pure realm of light and spirit. A Christian corollary necessarily entailed the fact that Christ didn't possess a real body since that would have enmeshed him in the material realm. Thus, in Christian

Gnosticism, the incarnation was not real; Christ only appeared to have a human body.

A certain proto-gnostic named Cerinthus lived in Ephesus and, according to Polycarp, was known to the Apostle John. Indeed, John denounced Cerinthus for his deviation from apostolic truth.[11] According to Cerinthus, the divine Christ-Spirit descended upon Jesus at baptism and rested upon him until the crucifixion, at which point it ascended back to the realm of light and left the human Jesus to die on the cross. On this understanding, Cerinthus and his fellow gnostics denied a true incarnation. When one reads John's Gospel and the Johannine Letters against this backdrop, their argument and purpose come into sharp focus. I select a few passages to illustrate the point.

John opens his first letter with a vivid and dramatic proclamation concerning the real incarnation of Jesus Christ. Note how John stresses that the apostles not only saw with their eyes the Word of life but actually touched him with their hands (1 John 1:2). He then returns to this point in chapter 4 where he warns his readers about the false prophets that have gone out into the world. They may be easily identified by this theological test: "Every spirit that acknowledges that Jesus Christ has come in the flesh is from God, but every spirit that does not acknowledge Jesus is not from God. This is the spirit of antichrist, which you have heard is coming and even now is already in the world" (1 John 4:2–3). He then concludes with a final affirmation of the reality of the incarnation in chapter 5. The quintessential Christian confession affirms that Jesus is the Son of God. The accent here falls on the human Jesus being the Son of God. This refutes the gnostic view that the Christ was a pure spirit who was not joined to true humanity. So that there can be no confusion on this point, John clearly spells out what he means by the following affirmation:

> This is the one who came by water and blood—Jesus Christ. He did not come by water only, but by water and blood. And it is the Spirit who testifies, because the Spirit is the truth. For there are three that testify: the Spirit,

---

11. This story is related by Irenaeus in *Adv. Haer.* III.3.4.

> the water and the blood; and the three are in agreement. We accept human testimony, but God's testimony is greater because it is the testimony of God, which he has given about his Son. Whoever believes in the Son of God accepts this testimony. Whoever does not believe God has made him out to be a liar, because they have not believed the testimony God has given about his Son. And this is the testimony: God has given us eternal life, and this life is in his Son. Whoever has the Son has life; whoever does not have the Son of God does not have life. (1 John 5:6–12).

The threefold testimony—water, blood, and Spirit—probably refers to Jesus's baptism at the outset of his ministry, when John the Baptist saw the Spirit descend upon Jesus (John 1:32–14), and the crucifixion as the crucial moment when the Son was glorified by the Father (John 12:23–33; 17:1–5; 19:34–35). Recall that a soldier pierced Jesus's side with a spear, "bringing a sudden flow of blood and water" (John 19:34). The point being made is that Jesus really died and possessed a real, human body. The Holy Spirit testifies to the reality of these two facts and thus forms a threefold witness to the truth of a genuine incarnation (cf. 2 Cor 13:1; Deut 19:15), not merely an appearance or charade, as various forms of Gnosticism would have it.

One could pursue this further, but enough has been discussed to demonstrate the ongoing validity of the theological test for false prophecy. Jesus, Paul, Peter, and John all warn of false prophets arising from within the fellowship of Jesus followers. They provide clear guidelines that demarcate boundaries of truth and error. Church history is littered with the tragic consequences of false prophecy and false teaching. The people of God must adhere to the truths revealed in Scripture.

The Ethical Test

The NT provides numerous examples of the ethical test. Jesus and his apostles place great weight on this litmus test for false prophets.

We begin with the Master's words drawing attention to behavior as a test of genuineness. As he concludes the Sermon on the Mount, Jesus pointedly warns his followers against false prophets. These "ferocious wolves" who dress in sheep's clothing will be known by their deeds (Matt 7:15–20).

The Apostle Paul had to deal with interlopers in the house churches of Corinth who claimed to be genuine apostles. Paul doesn't mince words: he calls them "false apostles, deceitful workers, masquerading as apostles of Christ" (2 Cor 11:13). Besides peddling false teaching (2 Cor 11:4), their behavior belies their bogus claims. They boast in the way the world does (11:18), exploit and take advantage of believers, push themselves forward, and even slap the Corinthians in the face (11:20)! Paul solemnly warns, "Their end will be what their actions deserve" (11:15). In what is probably his last letter shortly before his martyrdom, Paul gives his lieutenant Timothy a pointed warning about the behavior of false prophets and teachers (2 Tim 3:1–9). His indictment upon all such individuals is unambiguous: "They are men of depraved minds, who, as far as the faith is concerned, are rejected" (3:8).

The most devastating critique of false teachers' behavior, however, appears in the Apostle Peter's second letter (2 Pet 2). From a grocery list of misdeeds, note especially the following: depraved conduct, greed, disrespect for authority, arrogance, blasphemy, adultery, and love of money. Peter warns that those who follow such a course will experience certain and fearful judgment: "They too will perish. They will be paid back with harm for the harm they have done" (2:12–13).

The relevance of this test to our own time is readily apparent. A brief survey of prominent false teachers of the last forty years, including such notorious deceivers as Jim Jones, David Koresh, and Marshall Applegate, turns up dossiers that seem to come right from the descriptions of Jesus, Paul, Peter, and John. Behavior and character matter; indeed, they are the essential building blocks of holiness and righteousness, without which none will enter the kingdom of God. Evangelicals beware! Behavior must match belief. If it doesn't, there are legitimate grounds for alarm. "Not everyone who says to me, 'Lord, Lord,' will enter the kingdom of heaven, but only those who do the will of my Father who is in heaven. Many will say to me on that day, 'Lord, Lord, did we not prophesy in your name and in your name drive out demons and in your name perform many miracles?' Then I will tell them plainly, 'I never knew you. Away from me, you evildoers!'" (Matt 7:21–23).

The Holy Spirit

We have not, however, exhausted the resources available for discerning false prophecy. Clearly, another invaluable resource lies at hand for distinguishing truth from error. This may be called an inner conviction or anointing of the Holy Spirit that comes to the assistance of believers and guides them into the truth. In the words of Jesus as recorded in John's Gospel, "But when he, the Spirit of truth, comes, he will guide you into all the truth" (16:13). In my view, this assistance was already present during the old covenant era and to Jeremiah's generation, in particular. Jeremiah knew, as did the faithful remnant of his day, that what he said was true. They heard the inner voice of conviction and they trusted it. So it is in the new covenant era. In fact, the Apostle John explicitly mentions this special ministry of the Holy Spirit. I quote in full his statement:

> But you have an anointing from the Holy One, and all of you know the truth. I do not write to you because you do not know the truth, but because you do know it and because no lie comes from the truth. Who is the liar? It is whoever denies that Jesus is the Messiah. Such a person is the antichrist—denying the Father and the Son. No one who denies the Son has the Father; whoever acknowledges the Son has the Father also. (1 John 2:20–23)

At the end of the day, this is a word of hope for the church militant as it moves forward into the fray against false *isms*. The Lord knows his people and they know him. And he does not leave them to their own devices. He provides an inner voice, a moral and doctrinal compass that safeguards them against falsehood and error. The Apostle John's word to the young believers of his day resonates with Jeremiah's faithful witness to an earlier era: "You are strong, and the word of God lives in you, and you have overcome the evil one" (1 John 2:14).

5

Jeremiah's Complaints

INTRODUCTION

Some of the most fascinating and illuminating portions of the book of Jeremiah feature the prophet's complaints or laments. The fascination in these passages lies in the unprecedented nature of the outbursts. A faithful messenger levels bitter accusations against Yahweh for his unjust actions. The cheeky character of such an audacious charge is breathtaking. One recalls the protestations of the patriarchs against Yahweh's threatened judgment; Abraham pleads on behalf of Sodom and Gomorrah (Gen 18:16–33), Moses on behalf of rebellious Israel (Exod 32:9–14), but nowhere does either accuse him of outright wrongdoing.

The closest parallel to Jeremiah's complaints occurs in the book of Job. A righteous man, Job suffers a series of devastating disasters that reduce him to a shattered shell, bereft of family and possessions, afflicted with boils over his entire body and seated in a heap of ashes (Job 1:1—2:10). Remarkably, Job responds with this question: "Shall we accept good from God, and not trouble?" (2:10). In dialogue with his would-be comforters, however, he questions why God allowed him to be born in light of his subsequent suffering and sorrow. It would have been far better to have died at childbirth (3:11; 10:18–19). The aggrieved Jeremiah bitterly agrees: "Cursed be the day I was born! May the day my mother bore me not be blessed!" (Jer 20:14). At first, Job's criticism of God's governance is implied, not directly stated. But as the book of Job unfolds, the persistent accusation of Job's friends that he is a secret sinner takes its toll, and Job responds with increasing bitterness about God's dealings with him and vehemently protests his innocence. Furthermore, the disparity between the power and wisdom of God and human frailty and limitations frustrates Job to no end. He finally blurts out, "How then can I dispute with him? How can I find words to argue with him?" (9:14). Furthermore, says Job, "Even if I summoned him and he responded, I do not believe he would give me a hearing" (9:16; cf. 19:23–24; 23:3–5; 27:2–6; 31:35). Job's sufferings drive him to a truly unnerving verdict: "He destroys both the blameless and the wicked" (9:22).

Job and Jeremiah are fellow travelers on the road to Zion. Like Job, Jeremiah begins by questioning God's justice: "You are always righteous, LORD, when I bring a case before you. Yet I would speak with you about your justice" (Jer 12:1). He then takes his discontent further by accusing him of being "like a deceptive brook, like a spring that fails" (Jer 15:18). Finally, he gives vent to his deepest hurt and bluntly charges him with deception: "You deceived me, LORD, and I was deceived; you overpowered me and prevailed" (Jer 20:7). For both Job and Jeremiah, sustained, intense, personal suffering wears them down. The strain becomes almost unbearable as they sink into the depths of despair and recrimination. Whom else can they blame but the one who accomplishes all things according to his will against all opposition (Job 9; Jer 10:11–16; 11:17)?

There is one more biblical character who accuses God of not doing the right thing. That person is also a prophet, namely, Jonah. The immediate occasion for Jonah's accusation does not, however, arise out of a period of prolonged personal suffering but out of personal prejudice. Jonah hates the Ninevites, inhabitants of the capital city of the Assyrian Empire, for their cruelty and oppression. He wants God to punish them with catastrophic judgment.

But when God extends mercy to them in response to Jonah's preaching, the prophet is so angry that he tells God, "I wish I were dead" (Jonah 4:9). Jonah's patriotic nationalism has so blinded him to the wideness of God's mercy that he lashes out in anger against a gracious and compassionate God who "is slow to anger . . . and relents from sending calamity" (Jonah 4:2). This prophetic masterpiece is open-ended; we don't know if Jonah ever repented of his prejudice. Because it is open-ended, the story confronts the reader with the same choice Jonah faced, whether to repent or not. An angry Jonah describes our own deeply polarized nation and challenges our ingrained prejudices.

Job, Jonah, and Jeremiah all found fault with God's justice. Each one received his day in court to plead his case. In all three cases, of course, the fault lies not in Yahweh but in the distorted perceptions of the plaintiffs. The special contribution of Jeremiah's complaints lies in their remarkable honesty. Precisely in these tantrums we gain fresh insight into our own humanity as faithful followers of Christ. In short, much can be learned as we enter into Jeremiah's "dark night of the soul."[1]

AN OVERVIEW OF THE FIVE COMPLAINTS

We begin by listing in chart form the five complaints and summarizing the troubling questions that tortured Jeremiah.

---

1. This expression refers to an experience of spiritual desolation in which one feels there is no hope of consolation. The expression may be traced back to the sixteenth-century mystic St. John of the Cross, who wrote a poem that was later called *Dark Night of the Soul*. The experience of doubt in one's spiritual journey is a common theme and is voiced by many saints, such as St. Paul of the Cross in the eighteenth century and St. Thérèse of Liseux in the nineteenth. Perhaps best known is the dark night of St. Teresa of Calcutta. In the Protestant tradition, the Christian classic by John Bunyan describes a stage called "the slough of despond." Yancey describes several contemporary Christians who struggled with this phenomenon (*Soul Survivor*).

Text	Troubling Question
11:18—12:6	Why have you allowed my own kin and neighbors to devise assassination plots against me?
15:10–21	Why do I suffer for doing your will?
17:14–18	Why do you and my persecutors terrorize me?
18:19–23	Why don't you do something about those who plot to kill me?
20:7–18	Why must my messages always bring reproach and ridicule? Why was I ever born?

I think the most profitable way of approaching the complaints is to take them in canonical order. While not all would agree that the complaints are chronologically arranged, it seems most plausible to read them in such a fashion. The assumption is that they reveal Jeremiah's progressive descent into "the slough of despond" (Bunyan). Such a reading reveals illuminating insights into the psychology and theology of suffering and persecution. With that preliminary word, let's take a closer look at Jeremiah's complaints.

FIRST COMPLAINT (11:18—12:6)

Setting

The first complaint most likely arises after Jeremiah's initial forays into the public arena in which he gained instant notoriety for messages running against the grain of popular expectation. Most likely, the first complaint takes shape after the famous temple sermon (Jer 7). The oracles in chapters 2:1—11:17 throw light on the immediate circumstances surrounding Jeremiah's first complaint. In fact, Jeremiah's message immediately preceding the first complaint concludes with the affirmation that Yahweh himself planted his people (11:17). The first complaint is predicated on this indisputable fact (12:2).

Jeremiah's outburst followed hard on the heels of a shocking disclosure: Yahweh revealed to Jeremiah a plot against his life planned by his Anathoth neighbors. How many joined in this plot is not stated. What we do know is that the conspirators, who included even Jeremiah's relatives (12:6), warned him to stop prophesying in the name of Yahweh and that if he did not cease, they would put him to death (11:21). Jeremiah had been quite oblivious to their machinations. He never imagined they might be capable of such a deed (11:19). Presumably, the plotters objected to Jeremiah's prediction of the utter destruction of the temple (Jer 7:14). Given that Anathoth was an important priestly city, one can at least appreciate their alarm and anxiety should such a fate befall the temple. But murder? Self-interest leads people to extreme measures.

Yahweh then revealed to Jeremiah what would happen to the city of Anathoth. A disaster of unimaginable proportions would befall its citizens. Undoubtedly, this occurred during the Babylonian invasion of Nebuchadnezzar in 587–586 BC, "the year of their punishment" (11:23).[2]

The impact of this episode shook Jeremiah to the core. How could his fellow citizens and relatives among whom he had grown up resort to murder? Furthermore, how could a priestly city create an environment in which such behavior was even contemplated? It dawned on Jeremiah that he lived in the midst of hypocrites. When their self-interest was endangered, they could resort to criminal behavior without any qualms whatsoever. Jeremiah came to an unsettling conclusion: "The heart is deceitful above all things and beyond cure. Who can understand it?" (17:9). This realization provokes the first complaint.

Familiar Problem

Jeremiah's first complaint pursues a well-trodden line of inquiry. He would not be the first nor the last to raise the question of theodicy.[3] Theodicy (from Gk. *theos*, "god," and *dikē*, "justice")

---

2. Apparently, not all the citizens perished because 128 Jews from Anathoth returned from the exile with Zerubbabel (Ezra 2:23).

3. The problem of theodicy appears already in ancient Mesopotamian literature. Foster, "Babylonian Theodicy," 492–95.

concerns a long-standing problem of reconciling how a good and just God can permit (or even decree) evil in the world. No surprise then that biblical literature revisits this troubling feature of life. Once again, the book of Job provides the most obvious parallel to Jeremiah's complaint. However, two well-known psalms also take up this vexing issue, namely, Psalm 73, attributed to Asaph, and Psalm 37, ascribed to David. Both Psalms exhort the faithful not to be dismayed or fret over the prosperity of the wicked. The reason is that such prosperity is of limited duration and the wicked will eventually face terrifying judgment (Ps 37:1, 20, 28, 33, 35–36, 38; Ps 73:2–12, 17–20). Jeremiah revisits this conundrum, agitated by his own close encounter with death by assassination.

Flow of Argument

Let's follow the progression of Jeremiah's complaint in terms of its basic elements. Then we will be in a position to assess its claim and Yahweh's response.

- Complimentary opening: "You are always righteous . . ."
- Critical query: "Yet I would speak with you about your justice . . ."
- Charge (implied) of divine culpability: "Why does the way of the wicked prosper?"
- Case for divine culpability: "You have planted them . . ."
- Claim of innocence: "Yet you know me, LORD . . ."
- Call for immediate justice: "Drag them off . . ."

Jeremiah's complaint begins with a begrudging acknowledgment that Yahweh always prevails in matters of justice and righteousness. That does not, however, deter him from accusing Yahweh of injustice.[4] Acting as a prosecuting attorney, he argues that, in the final analysis, Yahweh bears some responsibility for the

---

4. "This text poses the problem of theodicy more frontally than any other OT text." Brueggemann, *To Pluck Up*, 112n8.

reprehensible acts of the wicked because it was he who permitted them to thrive in their waywardness. For their part, they profess loyalty but are in fact frauds. Jeremiah calls upon Yahweh to adjudicate between these hypocrites and him, an innocent sufferer. That leads Jeremiah to blurt out his own notion of how divine fairness and justice should be administered in the present situation: unsparing and immediate judgment upon his adversaries. What is particularly galling to Jeremiah is the smug confidence of the general population that Yahweh pays no attention to their behavior, whether good or bad.

Though not the primary point of Jeremiah's case against Yahweh, worth noting are his comments about the effect of immoral, rebellious behavior on the environment. Flora and fauna alike suffer the consequences of human misbehavior (12:4). The relevance of this for our own environmental woes should not be overlooked. The interconnectedness of all life on planet earth and the fragility of our ecosystems become more apparent every day. Human government must take seriously the moral demands of the God who created us in his image with an inherent sense of right and wrong. He also charged humanity with taking care of his creation, not abusing it (Gen 1:26–31; Ps 8:5–8). We ignore this mandate to our extreme peril.

God's Answer (12:5–17)

So, how does Yahweh respond to Jeremiah's complaint about his divine justice? This is a fascinating passage that invites careful reading and reflection. The response is twofold: first, a personal word directed to the prophet, and second, one concerning the people of Judah and her neighbors.

A Personal Word to Jeremiah (12:5–6)

Yahweh definitely does not coddle Jeremiah; he chides him for complaining and then, in effect, sternly warns him, "If you think it's tough now, I have news for you—it's going to get even tougher. So get used to it!"[5] Included in the warning is the shocking disclosure that even his relatives and family members have turned against him. He is put on guard not to trust them. One can only imagine the impact this had on Jeremiah. Any illusions that his prophesying would lead to national repentance and revival are quickly dispelled. In fact, as the rest of Yahweh's word to Jeremiah indicates, the outcome is both certain and catastrophic. No wonder Jeremiah is called "the weeping prophet."[6]

A National Word to Judah and Her Neighbors (12:7–17)

There is one constant running throughout the messages of Jeremiah: Yahweh has decreed judgment upon Judah for her covenant disobedience. Time is running out and the day of reckoning is at hand. The metaphors and images conveying this message are like a Mozart piano concerto: though it has ever-changing variations, it always returns to the major themes. In the passage before us, a number of images combine to depict Judah's impending desolation. Whether described in terms of house, inheritance, vineyard, or field, Yahweh's people have become to him like a threatening lion or a speckled bird of prey, provoking attacks by the rest of the birds. In fact, one may properly say that Jeremiah 12:7–17 constitutes Yahweh's complaint against his people. There can only be one outcome: "The sword of the LORD will devour from one end of the land to the other: no one will be safe" (12:12). Judah is not alone; all the other "wicked neighbors" will also be uprooted (12:14). As

---

5. Peterson takes the title of his book on Jeremiah (*Run with the Horses*) from this passage. "The thickets by the Jordan" or "the flooding of the Jordan" (TNIV text and footnote at 12:5) refers to the dense undergrowth surrounding the channel in which the Jordan winds its way southward to the Dead Sea. Trying to make one's way through this brush is an exhausting enterprise.

6. "The grief of Jeremiah was at two levels. First, it was a grief he grieved for the end of his people. And that was a genuine grief because he cared about this people and he knew God cared about this people. But the second dimension of his grief, more intense, was because no one would listen and no one would see what was so transparent to him." Brueggemann, *Prophetic Imagination*, 47.

a matter of fact, the Babylonian invasions did wreak havoc upon all the little nation-states in the land bridge between Mesopotamia and Egypt (Ammon, Moab, Edom, Phoenicia, Philistia, and the Aramean states). There is, however, even for these peoples, a glimmer of hope in the future. If they adopt the faith of Israel, they will be restored. I return to this message of eschatological hope in the last chapter.

SECOND COMPLAINT (15:10-21)

Setting

The second complaint occurs sometime later. A period of time must have elapsed since it follows the symbolic act of the linen belt, a sign-act requiring several months at least for completion (13:1-11). In addition, we learn of a drought, alluded to in 14:1. Jeremiah's second complaint arises from his anger over the false prophets and their steady barrage of false promises: "The prophets keep telling them, 'You will not see the sword or suffer famine. Indeed, I will give you lasting peace in this place'" (14:13). His anguish is exacerbated by two harsh realities: the majority of citizens believe the false prophets, and nothing he can do or say will avert divine judgment: "Even if Moses and Samuel were to stand before me, my heart would not go out to this people. Send them away from my presence! Let them go!" (15:1). With words recalling a divorce formula, Yahweh turns his back on Judah (cf. Hos 1:9; 2:2). Furthermore, Yahweh repeatedly forbids Jeremiah from interceding for the people (7:16; 11:14; 14:11). Making matters even more agonizing, Yahweh commands Jeremiah that if the people ask him where they can go to escape, he is to offer them only the following grim outcomes: death, sword, starvation, or captivity (15:2).[7] Imagine their response to what Jeremiah claims is a word from

---

7. The reader may recall that the elder John alludes to this Jeremiah passage in his description of the four horsemen of the Apocalypse (Rev 6:1-8) and actually quotes it in his depiction of the beast out of the sea (Rev 13:10).

Yahweh! They spew out their utter contempt for Jeremiah's seemingly heartless response to their frantic inquiries.

Jeremiah is deeply agitated. He can endure it no longer. His quarrel with Yahweh erupts in another complaint.[8] As with the first complaint, we analyze the second in terms of its component parts and then make some comments on the content.

Structure

Text	Literary Form
15:10	Lament
15:11–12	Divine response: deliverance oracle
15:13–14	Divine judgment oracle
15:15	Personal petition
15:16–17	Personal testimony affirming righteous behavior
15:18	Lament and accusation
15:19–21	Divine response: call for repentance and a deliverance oracle

Substance of Complaint

Jeremiah begins with a lament he shares with Job—he wishes he had never been born. His life is totally consumed with controversy. That he is reviled has nothing to do with money: "I have neither lent nor borrowed," he says, "yet everyone curses me" (v. 10b). Instead, it is his message that offends—having very much to do with politics! Perhaps none of the prophets experienced such widespread contempt as Jeremiah (he describes himself as "a man with whom the whole land strives and contends"). This crushes the spirit as surely as physical ailments.

What he needed the most he received: an encouraging word from Yahweh, who promises to deliver him from the hand of his

---

8. "Jeremiah had a midlife crisis and in one of his laments asked Yahweh for vengeance on his persecutors because he was bearing reproach for carrying out his prophetic mission." Lundbom, *Prophet Like Moses*, 13.

enemies (15:11). To this is added a word of exhortation by way of a proverbial question: who can break iron or bronze? This harkens back to Jeremiah's initial call in which Yahweh said he would make Jeremiah like "an iron pillar and a bronze wall to stand against the whole land" (Jer 1:18). To paraphrase the point: "Jeremiah, I made you tough, you can do this!"[9]

But Jeremiah doesn't feel tough, he feels vulnerable. Yahweh doesn't appreciate the personal cost involved in the mission. Jeremiah reminds Yahweh of his devotion and behavior, bespeaking a person who takes seriously the demands of the Sinai covenant and what it means to be a member of God's elect, holy people. Jeremiah's language in 15:16–17 recalls the opening psalm of the Psalter, which describes the way of the righteous in contrast to the way of the wicked (Ps 1:1–2). Therein lies the nub of Jeremiah's persecution. Few of his fellow countrymen care a fig about the demanding standards of Sinai. Their behavior deeply offends Jeremiah, causing him to withdraw from their company and further widening the gulf between them. Jeremiah's righteous indignation over their rebellion mirrors that of Yahweh, who denounces the people for their faithlessness.

The upshot is predictable: constant abuse and ridicule, exacting a heavy emotional toll. Jeremiah protests over his plight without a solution. He lashes out at Yahweh with an impetuous accusation: "You deceived and failed me"![10]

---

9. In *The Message* Peterson paraphrases 1:8 as "I'm making you as impregnable as a castle, immovable as a steel post, solid as a concrete block wall. You're a one-man defense system against this culture . . . They'll fight you, but they won't even scratch you. I'll back you up every inch of the way.' GOD'S Decree."

10. The word picture employed by Jeremiah may not immediately connect with readers who live in well-watered parts of the world. In the land of Israel there are extremely arid portions with less than five inches of rainfall annually. Even in areas receiving twenty-plus inches a year, the distribution of rain is quite sharply divided into a rainy season (October–April) and a dry season (May–September). During the dry season a number of streams and springs dry up until the ensuing rainy season. Jeremiah, like his contemporaries, was attuned to the rhythm of life in the land of two seasons. He was, as Lundbom points out, "a keen observer of nature and the created order" (*Prophet*

Jeremiah's Complaints

Does Jeremiah lodge a valid complaint? What truth is there in the twofold charge that Yahweh both deceived and failed him? The problem we encounter is one of perception. Obviously, Jeremiah had a different expectation for the outcome of his preaching than what actually occurred. Did he think Yahweh had promised something more promising? Yahweh certainly gave Jeremiah no glowing promises of repentance and revival. From the outset he made it abundantly clear that the die was cast and Judah would be overthrown and dispossessed because of her covenant disobedience. Nonetheless, Jeremiah might have harbored some faint hope for an eleventh-hour reprieve—after all, the Ninevites repented and were spared after Jonah's announcement of imminent judgment. Be that as it may, Jeremiah could never have anticipated the ferocity of the hatred directed against him. In reality, this level of animosity can scarcely be imagined until one confronts it head-on. Yahweh did not spell out the intensity of the pushback against Jeremiah personally; he simply told his prophet to stand against them and never give in. Now it's beginning to sink in—Jeremiah realizes just how difficult it's going to be. But is Yahweh guilty of deception and of failing Jeremiah? Should he have informed Jeremiah in detail? One must first ask, Are prophets (or believers) entitled to this kind of information? There may well be good and sufficient reasons for Yahweh *not* to inform his spokespersons of all the personal suffering lying ahead. As Jesus said, "Each day has enough trouble of its own" (Matt 6:34). Furthermore, one doubts the wisdom of revealing beforehand all the sufferings a person must endure. The psychological burden of such awareness would likely be emotionally crippling. Though it may sound trite, it comes down to the sentiment of a well-known hymn: "trust and obey, for there's no other way."

Like Moses, 19). Jeremiah's reference is to an unexpected situation in which a normally reliable spring or stream, owing to below-normal rainfall, dries up. For shepherds and farmers depending on it, the consequences could be devastating.

Speech of Yahweh

Once again, Yahweh's response to this outburst merits careful attention. The first word to Jeremiah is a direct summons to repent of such unworthy accusations. In fact, immediate repentance is a prerequisite for further service as a spokesman. Second, Yahweh reminds him that no compromise can be countenanced. Under no circumstances may Jeremiah turn to them (i.e., overlook their disobedience); they must turn to him (i.e., respond to his message by repenting and reforming their ways). Third, Yahweh promises both to fortify Jeremiah for the continuing conflict and to rescue him from his wicked and cruel enemies. To his credit, Jeremiah repented and stayed the course.

An instructive parallel occurs in the teaching of Jesus. He told his disciples that servants who work all day in the fields are still expected to prepare their master's meal before their own and that when they do so, they should not expect a special word of thanks. Jesus's climactic saying throws light on Jeremiah's complaint: "So you also, when you have done everything you were told to do, should say, 'We are unworthy servants; we have only done our duty'" (Luke 17:10). In short, the task assigned by Yahweh may be demanding and dangerous, but at the end of the day, we are expected to do our duty and not complain about our lot. Few of us have really come to grips with this kingdom principle; we spend far too much time in the complaint department.

THIRD COMPLAINT (17:14-18)

Setting

The third complaint follows sometime after Jeremiah's symbolic action whereby he forgoes marriage and withdraws from important social functions such as funerals and weddings (16:1-18). The jarring nature of Jeremiah's behavior and his even-more-shocking explanation for it lead predictably to increased abuse. One hears in the third complaint Jeremiah's deep personal pain.

He also complains about his sense of terror—terror caused by both enemies and Yahweh. Why he feels terror at the hand of Yahweh is puzzling and requires further inquiry. But first we lay out the structure of this passage.

Structure

Text	Literary Form
17:14	Petition for healing and deliverance
17:15	Report of ridicule
17:16	Protest of innocence
17:17	Petition and confession of trust
17:18	Petition for punishment of enemies and personal deliverance

Substance

The third complaint opens with a cry for personal healing. What was the nature of the malady? Whatever it was, the disorder doubtless originated in the intense psychological distress and grief of the prophet. As is well known, a number of physical problems are psychosomatic. Coupled with this petition for healing is a prayer for personal deliverance. Once again the assumed background of this request is the constant threat of assassination. As we have already rehearsed, Yahweh preserved Jeremiah through a number of close calls.

A new element enters his complaints. We overhear a taunt by his opponents, who jeer at him because his oft-repeated warnings of divine judgment upon the city and temple have gone unfulfilled. No doubt his adversaries appealed to this as evidence that Jeremiah was a false prophet.

Jeremiah responds with a protest to Yahweh concerning his unjust treatment. He reminds Yahweh that he has remained steadfast to his calling to be a shepherd of his people, even though that often entailed the unpleasant task of speaking the truth in love (cf.

Eph 4:15). One thing is certain: he does not wish for the judgment he keeps announcing. Reading between the lines, we may assume that his opponents were accusing him of desiring Judah's destruction. Jeremiah rests his case with Yahweh, who knows his heart (17:10).

Jeremiah then petitions Yahweh not to terrorize him, especially since he is counting on Yahweh to preserve his life in the coming national catastrophe (17:17). So what does Jeremiah mean by this terror from Yahweh? Probably it's the horror of Judah's imminent punishment emanating from Yahweh himself. Jeremiah is struggling with the realization that he will be right in the thick of this looming national disaster, and that creates a sense of dread and fear: How can he possibly survive? Jeremiah needs reassurance that Yahweh will indeed be his refuge.

This leads Jeremiah to petition Yahweh to pour out on his persecutors their due recompense, described as shame, terror, and "double destruction" (17:18). A difficult ethical and moral question arises. Didn't Jesus and the apostles teach a quite different approach to enemies? The short answer is yes (Matt 5:38–48; Acts 7:60; Rom 12:14, 17, 19; 1 Pet 3:9). The new covenant in Christ does raise the bar in terms of expected behavior: "Be perfect, therefore, as your heavenly Father is perfect" (Matt 5:48)—a high standard indeed! Christians are deeply divided, however, on the question of whether praying for the destruction of national enemies is ever sanctioned.[11]

The fact that there is no divine response to Jeremiah's complaint is noteworthy. This silence in itself suggests that Jeremiah's petition is misguided. Of course, Yahweh will indeed punish his wayward people, but not in response to Jeremiah's personal

---

11. I am aware of only one NT reference that might be interpreted as an instance where believers prayed for the judgment of their persecutors. During the fifth seal judgment the martyrs cry out to the Lord, "How long, Sovereign Lord, holy and true, until you judge the inhabitants of the earth and avenge our blood?" (Rev 6:10). But note carefully that the petition is in the form of a question about timing, not a request that it be carried out. On the larger issue of war and a Christian response to it, see Hays, *Moral Vision of the New Testament*.

petition to do so. Judgment and salvation rest with Yahweh alone, and no mortal messenger controls the levers of divine providence, whether for weal or for woe. For this we can all be profoundly grateful.

FOURTH COMPLAINT (18:19-23)

Setting

The fourth complaint follows Jeremiah's visit to the potter where he watches a marred vessel being refashioned (18:1-10). This leads to an intense sermon announcing divine disaster upon Judah and Jerusalem (18:11-17). The reaction of the listeners is totally disheartening. They formulate a twofold strategy to deal with this troublemaker, namely, attack him verbally and "pay no attention to anything he says" (18:18). This prompts Jeremiah's fourth complaint.

Structure

The following table outlines the flow of Jeremiah's complaint.

Text	Literary Form
18:19	Appeal and protest on account of unjust accusations
18:20a	Rhetorical question emphasizing the unfairness of the accusers
18:20b	Appeal for personal vindication
18:21-22a	Petition for sweeping judgment on men, women, and children
18:22b	Rationale for such drastic judgment: plots against the prophet
18:23a	Assurance of personal vindication
18:23bc	Petition for irreversible judgment

Substance

The Judeans double down on their verbal assaults against Jeremiah. This steady barrage of abuse fractures his fragile ego. In addition, plots against his life continue unabated (18:23). The injustice of it all, with no apparent recourse, drives him once again to plead his case before the divine judge. Surely Yahweh is not oblivious to their spiteful wrongdoing. What galls Jeremiah is the fact that he has gone to the wall for them. That is, despite Yahweh's insistence that he not intercede for the nation, Jeremiah has done precisely that, as Moses and Samuel might have (15:1). But their stubborn resistance is the last straw. The prophet lashes out in rage and presumes to tell Yahweh what he must do with the miscreants.[12]

Once again, notably, there is no divine response to this outburst. The silences of God are at times as instructive as his utterances. Jeremiah's rants have turned rancid. But to his credit, he stays the course. He probably came to the realization that what he said was just plain stupid—best forgotten and not repeated. So why, in God's providence, are such passages found in Scripture? Elementary pedagogy instructs us that we often learn from mistakes, from things we shouldn't do. Of course, correct models of behavior carry even greater potential for instruction, but negative examples still play a role. Furthermore, we need to be reminded that when hard times descend upon us, we are not experiencing something hitherto unknown in human experience. Rare indeed is the situation having no analogy whatsoever. In Jeremiah we encounter a person with whom we can relate in our own personal struggles. There is spiritual (and even therapeutic) value in reliving the hardships and low points of a fellow traveler, especially one who fights through the crisis and comes out still trusting in the God who is

---

12. In this we hear echoes of Jonah's angry response to Yahweh's mercy upon the people of Nineveh (Jonah 4:1–4). "Our compulsive timetables collide with God's leisurely providence. We tell God not only what to do but when to do it. We take him seriously—why else would we be praying?—but we take ourselves more seriously, telling him exactly what he must do for us and when." Peterson, *Run with the Horses*, 98.

there. Jeremiah was a survivor. May his life and witness assist us all to be spiritual survivors!

FIFTH COMPLAINT (20:7–18)

Setting

Sometime after visiting the potter, Jeremiah is instructed to buy a jar and go out to the Potsherd Gate near the Hinnom Valley. In the presence of some elders and priests, he carries out a dramatic, symbolic action depicting the shattering of Judah (19:1–15). Jeremiah then leaves the scene of the ghastly Topheth and proceeds to the temple courts. There he rains down upon his listeners another hellfire and brimstone sermon, announcing utter disaster upon Jerusalem and its surrounding villages. Pashhur, one of the priests in charge of the temple, is fed up with Jeremiah's constant harangues. He decides to beat some sense into this headstrong prophet who marches to the beat of his own drum. He has Jeremiah arrested, beaten, and placed in stocks overnight at the Upper Benjamin Gate, an extremely painful, humiliating punishment. The next day, when Pashhur releases Jeremiah from the stocks, he expects him to sing a different tune. Far from it! Speaking in the name of Yahweh, Jeremiah gives Pashhur an ominous nickname, "Terror on Every Side," a moniker anticipating his fate and that of his friends in the coming invasion. After surviving the horrors of the invasion, they are destined to die and be buried in Babylon (20:3–6). We don't know the immediate sequel to this clash. Did Pashhur return Jeremiah to the stocks or let him go? Whatever the case, the stocks episode probably triggered Jeremiah's final outburst.

Structure

The following table outlines the flow of Jeremiah's complaint.

Text	Literary Form
20:7	Accusation against Yahweh
20:8	Grounds for accusation
20:9	Aggravating circumstances
20:10	Report of a smear campaign
20:11	Praise to Yahweh
20:12	Petition for vengeance on persecutors
20:13	Praise to Yahweh
20:14	Curse upon his birthday
20:15–17	Curse upon the messenger of Jeremiah's birth
20:18	Final Lament

Substance

Probably the most striking feature of this final complaint is the emotional roller coaster the reader experiences. It's like listening to a person suffering from bipolar disorder. Jeremiah's outburst runs a whole gamut of emotions: from blessing to cursing, from despair to praise, from forgiveness to vengeance. On one hand, he accuses Yahweh of deception and unjust treatment; on the other, he sings praises to Yahweh for his constant presence and deliverance from enemies. But above all, we sense that Jeremiah is almost at the end of his rope. He is angry, bitter, and, seemingly, without hope. If ever there were a candidate for suicide, he fits the profile.

Let's examine more closely the specifics. He begins with a familiar accusation: Yahweh deceived him. We've suggested above that the charge of deception relates primarily to the degree and extent of the hostility directed against the prophet. The problem, as Jeremiah analyzes it, is that Yahweh's word comes upon him with such compulsion he has no choice; he must proclaim it.[13] But when he does, that invariably generates even more antagonism and hatred. For one possessed of a sensitive spirit, this vicious cycle

---

13. The Apostle Paul expresses a similar conviction about preaching the gospel: "Woe to me if I do not preach the gospel!" (1 Cor 9:16).

JEREMIAH'S COMPLAINTS

spins him well out of his comfort zone. The fact that a majority of his compatriots hate him with a passion hurts him deeply, and he becomes a wounded prophet.[14]

Inner turmoil leads Jeremiah to consider a radical option (20:9). What if he simply resigns and walks away? Why continue to bang his head against a wall? Surely he has stayed with it long enough. It's clear that the people of Judah have determined to persist in their wicked ways regardless of what he says or does. Who could blame him for quitting such a thankless job? The problem is that every time he seriously considers that option, the word of Yahweh bursts into flame and he can't extinguish it. He simply must proclaim the coming judgment.

Compounding matters, Jeremiah learns he is the victim of a smear campaign (20:10). The phrase "terror on every side" is now being pinned on Jeremiah. Recall that earlier Jeremiah had given that grim nickname to the priest Pashhur (20:3–4). One wonders if his enemies began taunting him with an epithet of his own making. Perhaps he became widely known about town as "terror on every side," illustrating what he means when he speaks of being ridiculed all day long, mocked, and insulted.

What is particularly disheartening for Jeremiah is the attitude of his so-called friends. They remind us of Job's useless comforters in his period of deep affliction and suffering (Job 16:2). In fact, Jeremiah's friends are not only secretly hoping he is wrong, but they are planning their revenge for when he is discredited as a true prophet. With friends like that, who needs enemies?

In the face of this disillusionment, Jeremiah reaffirms his trust in Yahweh's powerful presence and ultimate vindication (20:11). How edifying if that were the end of matters. One could rest content knowing that he was finally at peace.

Alas, such is not the case. He then petitions Yahweh to allow him to witness vengeance upon his persecutors (20:12b). As already discussed in the fourth complaint, such an attitude is sub-Christian and should not serve as an example to follow under

---

14. *Wounded Prophet* is the title of a biography of Henri Nouwen by Michael Ford. Jeremiah and Nouwen shared much in common.

the new covenant. There is no word of Yahweh that sanctions this vengeful attitude on the part of his disgruntled prophet. This is not Jeremiah's finest hour.

Unexpectedly, the prophet breaks out in rapturous praise: "Sing praise to the LORD!" (20:13). He seems to experience an emotional and spiritual breakthrough. Rather than demanding vengeance, he rejoices in Yahweh's rescue. The improvement in outlook, however, is short-lived.

With another drastic mood change, Jeremiah plummets to the bottom of the pit (20:14-18). He gives vent to blackest despair and venom, spewing out two fearful curses. The first curse falls on the day of his birth.[15] Though at the time it was viewed as a blessed day, he wants it remembered as a cursed one. Then, in a fit of spleen, he places a curse on the anonymous bearer of the good news of his birth and spitefully requests that the man suffer the same fate as the notorious citizens of Sodom and Gomorrah (Gen 19). Jeremiah's lame defense for his reprehensible behavior amounts to this: he failed to kill me in the womb (20:17)! Such ravings must be chalked up to a totally distraught and temporarily deranged prophet. Our discomfort at reading them is only increased by the absence of any divine response.

The succeeding chapter fast-forwards the narrative to the times of Zedekiah, the last king of Judah. From this I conclude that Jeremiah's last complaint is not indicative of his final disposition. Given the rather extensive account of the post-destruction era and Jeremiah's role in it (chs. 40-44), I assume that he snapped out of his despondency and regained his spiritual equilibrium. That should provide encouragement and hope for all of us. There is light at the end of our dark tunnel. With the God who is there, such optimism is not mere sentiment, it's conviction: "being sure of what we hope for and certain of what we do not see" (Heb 11:1).

---

15. Lundbom calls attention to the fact that Jeremiah does not go so far as to curse God or his parents, both actions being tantamount to blasphemy and hence a capital crime under the Sinai covenant (*Prophet Like Moses*, 110-11).

SIGNIFICANCE OF JEREMIAH'S COMPLAINTS

Of the many applications one could draw from Jeremiah's complaints, I single out one that seems especially relevant for our North American culture. American Christianity is permeated by a gospel message that sugarcoats the meaning of taking up one's cross and following in the steps of the savior. The prevailing message, particularly in our megachurch era, triumphantly proclaims that following Jesus is the way to be happy, healthy, wealthy, and wise. If one really believes in Jesus, then good things are bound to happen, and if not, then one simply needs to have more faith. Admittedly, this may be somewhat overstated, but the sad fact is large numbers of pastors and parishioners have bought into a rose-tinted, Pollyanna version of the good news.[16] One doesn't hear much about the struggles of a Jeremiah. It's almost as if to acknowledge such would be an admission of defeat. Furthermore, such "negative" preaching is not uplifting and certainly not what people want to hear. By all means, be upbeat and optimistic because that is what fills large auditoriums and sanctuaries—and results in larger revenues!

The dark night of the soul, the bitter disappointments of life, the anger and resentments that flood into our hearts, and even the attempted (and, tragically, sometimes successful) suicides that occur among those who confess Jesus as Lord, represent a much more prevalent reality than most are willing to admit.

Pastors and teachers are charged to proclaim the full counsel of God, including the spiritual struggles that are inherently a part of following Jesus. Only then can we recover a truly authentic Christian life.[17] The NT, when not cherry-picked, contains numerous passages that force us to confront the difficulties of discipleship and the sufferings of this life (e.g., Matt 13:20–21; Acts 14:22;

---

16. According to *Christianity Today*, the prosperity gospel is taught from the pulpit in about 38 percent of evangelical churches. Smietana, "Prosperity Gospel Taught."

17. I highly recommend Philip Yancey's book *Soul Survivor* as a wake-up call, reminding us that we are all dysfunctional, flawed travelers on the way to Zion. We all live east of Eden in this life, with bright hope for tomorrow in the restored Eden (Rev 22:1–5).

2 Cor 4:8–12; 11:23–30; 1 Thess 3:3; Heb 10:32–39; Jas 1:2–3; 1 Pet 1:6–7). The book of Psalms is a rich repository of laments recalling desperate crises, deep suffering, and difficult struggles. It seems to me that earlier generations of Christians had a much better handle on this reality. For example, in John Bunyan's spiritual masterpiece, *The Pilgrim's Progress*, the Slough of Despond is a frequented spot on the road to the heavenly Mt. Zion, and spiritual journals from a host of believers down the ages underscore the same point. In short, Jeremiah's complaints are required reading for all who take seriously Jesus's warning: "In this world you will have trouble. But take heart! I have overcome the world" (John 16:33). Listen again to Yahweh's initial summons to Jeremiah: "Get yourself ready!" (Jer 1:17).

One should not conclude, however, that Jeremiah the "weeping prophet" is only gloom and doom. Quite the contrary, there are a number of passages that radiate with bright hope for tomorrow.[18] That will be our focus in the final chapter.

---

18. "Jeremiah was a great prophet of hope, a message not simply tacked on to soften the judgment, or to bring his preaching legacy to a good conclusion. It was a bona fide message announced already in his word of call . . ." Lundbom, *Prophet Like Moses*, 147.

6

Jeremiah's Vision of the Future

Earlier, I called attention to the fact that a majority of Jeremiah's oracles are prophecies of judgment. Nonetheless, sprinkled throughout his dire pronouncements, one catches here and there "a gleam of glory bright."[1] These hopeful passages will be the focus of our study in this concluding chapter.

INTRODUCTORY MATTERS

Categories

At the outset, it's helpful to categorize the various kinds of prophecies falling under the heading "eschatological prophecies." By "eschatological" I mean that the fulfillment of a given prophecy is envisioned as future to the time of the prophet.[2] The degree of

---

1. The phrase is from the final stanza of Johnson Oatman Jr.'s hymn, "Higher Ground." Employing a different metaphor, Keown and Scalise observe, "The Book of Consolation stands as a refuge amid the storm of divine wrath that blows through the rest of the book of Jeremiah" (*Jeremiah 26-52*, 83).

2. Most OT prophecy is not prediction but proclamation. The latter is essentially preaching aimed at exhortation, condemnation, consolation, and encouragement. Proclamation may occasionally include prediction. Eschatology is derived from two Greek words, *eschatos*, meaning "last, final, or end," and

futurity could be short-term or long-term, and differentiating between the two is not always easy. "Jeremiah had two 'horizons' in view: the nearer horizon of the return of the exiles to Judah and the farther horizon of the regathering of Israel in the end times from the nations of the earth."[3] Interpreters disagree on what is near and what is far. I offer my determinations and let the reader decide for herself.

Addressees

Another important distinction concerns the primary people group to whom a given eschatological prophecy refers. Most of Jeremiah's prophecies are addressed to his contemporaries, the people of Judah. Characteristic of Jeremiah's preaching, however, is his emphasis upon the *entire house of Israel*, that is, both the northern and southern kingdoms.[4] His grand vision of future restoration includes the historical twelve-tribe federation that Yahweh constituted as his elect people at Mt. Sinai (Exod 19, 24). Judah's future blessedness does not occur without the northern tribes. Yahweh intends to restore all the tribes of Jacob, not simply the tribe of Judah.

Scope

The scope of Jeremiah's preaching, however, is even more inclusive. Recall that his prophetic call appointed him as "a prophet to the nations" (1:4). Several eschatological prophecies concern Judah's Levantine neighbors. In fact, chapters 46–51 form a block of material, often referred to as "Oracles against the Nations,"

logos, meaning "word, saying, or teaching." For a helpful discussion defending an eschatological approach to these prophecies, see Dearman, *Jeremiah and Lamentations*, 267–71

3. Wiersbe, *Be Decisive*, 128.

4. Jeremiah is not unique among the writing prophets in this regard, but he places more emphasis upon it than almost all the others except for the two Major Prophets Isaiah and Ezekiel.

containing messages directed to Egypt, Philistia, Moab, Ammon, Edom, Damascus, Kedar, Hazor, and Babylon.[5] Whereas most of the oracles are judgment oracles, a promise of national restoration is held out for Egypt (46:26), Moab (48:42), Ammon (49:6), and Elam (49:19). There is a wideness in God's mercy.

Arrangement

Sprinkled throughout the book of Jeremiah are a few snippets of eschatological hope. I will provide a brief summary of these passages. For the most part, however, Jeremiah gathers his salvation oracles into one block, similar to his block of prophecies against the nations. Chapters 30–33 are widely recognized as a distinctive unit focusing on the restoration of Israel. This block of material has been appropriately labeled "the Book of Consolation."

Leading Themes and Central Idea

Four main ideas hold these prophecies together:

- Regathering of Israel to the ancestral homeland
- Restoration of national life
- Renewal of spiritual life
- Reign of a Davidic king

Jeremiah's treatment of these four themes in redemptive history is a major contribution to biblical theology. But the central idea that actualizes these saving events is the institution of a new covenant. *This is the single most important concept Jeremiah proclaims.* He and his contemporary Ezekiel (also a priest) laid the groundwork for the all-important notion of the new covenant instituted by Jesus (Mark 14:22–26; Matt 26:26–30; Luke 22:14–20).

---

5. Isaiah contains blocks of prophecies against the nations (Isa 13–21, 23–24, 46–47). Ezekiel has the same (Ezek 25–32, 35; 38–39). See also Amos 1:3—2:5 and Zech 9:1–8. Kedar and Hazor were probably small states in the Arabian peninsula.

THE LIFE AND WITNESS OF JEREMIAH

VARIOUS ESCHATOLOGICAL PROPHECIES

I turn first to two passages outside the Book of Consolation in which we encounter prophecies with a silver lining. Assigning relative dates is precarious, but in all likelihood 3:14-18 comes from the early phases of Jeremiah's ministry (cf. Jer 3:6).

Jeremiah 3:14-18: Faithless Israel Returns to Zion

This text summarizes in a nutshell the essential message of restoration more fully unpacked in the Book of Consolation. The following outline traces the flow of the passage:

1. Call to return (v. 14a)
2. Choice of a remnant (v. 14b)
3. Provision of sound leadership (v. 15)
4. Ark of the covenant no longer missed (v. 16)
5. Jerusalem a center of worldwide pilgrimage (v. 17a)
6. People of Israel confirmed in righteousness (v. 17b)
7. Consolidation of all Israel in the land (v. 18)

Several items deserve comment. The use of husband-wife imagery to portray the relationship between Yahweh and Israel is not unique to Jeremiah. At least a century before Jeremiah, Hosea, a northern prophet from Israel, made telling use of this metaphor. Hosea depicts Yahweh as divorcing his wife Israel because of covenant unfaithfulness, a reality mirrored in the prophet's own failed marriage (see Hos 1-3). The good news is that "afterward the Israelites will return and seek the LORD their God and David their king" (Hos 4:5). Jeremiah shares the same hope.

The reference to "shepherds after my own heart" should be understood as referring to civil leaders like judges and kings. The term *shepherd* was widely used in the Ancient Near East to refer to political leaders.[6] The point of Jeremiah's prophecy is that one

---

6. Cf. Jer 10:21; 12:10; 22:22; 23:1-2; 25:34-36; 50:6; Isa 56:11; Ezek 34:2-10; Mic 5:2, 4; Nah 3:18; Zech 10:3; 11:5, 8.

day leaders will arise who truly care for their people as a shepherd cares for his sheep. This will be a welcome relief from the oppressive and spiritually bankrupt leadership of monarchs like Manasseh and Jeremiah's contemporaries Jehoiakim, Jehoiachin, and Zedekiah.

The reference to the ark of the covenant is intriguing. Apparently, sometime during Jeremiah's lifetime, the ark disappeared, a loss mourned by the people, especially those in a priestly village like Anathoth. The last biblical reference to the ark occurs in 2 Chronicles 35:3, Josiah's eighteenth year (ca. 622 BC). In this text Josiah restores the ark to its proper place in the holy of holies and insists it not be carried about on the shoulders of the Levites. This implies that during the days of the wicked King Manasseh, the ark had been removed from the temple, perhaps being displayed as a sort of icon possessing magical powers. Presumably, when Jeremiah was still young, the ark was present in the holy of holies. Mysteriously, there is no reference in the OT to the ark thereafter, except for Jeremiah's comment that it would not be missed "in those days" (i.e., the last days), nor to its being taken by Nebuchadnezzar when he carried off the "articles of value from the temple" (2 Chr 36:10) in the days of Jehoiachin. Neither is there any mention of it later when Nebuchadnezzar destroyed the temple and "carried to Babylon all the articles from the temple of God, both large and small, and the treasures of the LORD's temple..." (2 Chr 36:18; cf. 1 Esd 1:54).

Jewish scholars have long debated when the ark disappeared from the holy of holies and who was responsible for its disappearance. According to rabbis Eliezer and Yohai, the ark was carried off to Babylon by Nebuchadnezzar. Neither of them speculate on its ultimate fate (*b. Yoma* 53b).[7] Other Jewish traditions preserve differing explanations. In the Mishnah there is a tradition that the ark was hidden under the pavement of the chamber of wood in the Court of Israel (*m. Yoma* 6:1).[8] Rabbi Nahman repeats this

---

7. The Babylonian Talmud was completed in the fifth century AD.

8. The Mishnah was codified around AD 200 and includes traditions from the time of Jesus and earlier.

tradition (*b. Yoma* 54a). According to another tradition, Josiah hid the ark beneath the holy of holies, which today is probably directly under the Islamic shrine called the Dome of the Rock (*y. Šeqal.* 49c). An earlier tradition, preserved in the apocryphal work 2 Maccabees, claims that Jeremiah took the ark and buried it on Mt. Nebo (in modern-day Jordan).[9] This tradition, however, is hard to square with what Jeremiah says about the ark in 3:16.[10]

So, how should Christians respond to this mystery? Whether the ark still exists and is beneath the temple mount is a fascinating historical question,[11] but one lacking theological significance for Christians inasmuch as the NT teaching is quite clear: the body of Christ is the new temple whose destiny is not linked in any way to the fortunes of the historical ark (1 Cor 3:16; 6:19; 2 Cor 6:16; Eph 2:19–22; 1 Pet 2:5).[12] Nor, in my opinion, should Christians get on the bandwagon to advocate for a third temple. If a third temple were to exist, then bad things likely would happen there, the Scriptures suggest (Mark 13:14–19; Matt 24:15–21; 2 Thess 2:4; Rev 11:1–14). Furthermore, seeking to contribute to the building of a third temple is counterproductive in bringing about a

9. See 2 Macc 2:1–8. Second Maccabees was written sometime between 104 and 63 BC.

10. For an embarrassing account of a modern, misguided "arkeologist" who illegally attempted to "discover" the ark on Mt. Nebo, see Helyer, *Mountaintop Theology*, 74.

11. Religious Jews belonging to an organization called the Temple Institute believe the ark is indeed buried beneath the Temple Mount. See Helyer, *Mountaintop Theology*, 75n10, for a brief account of a foiled attempt by two former Israeli chief rabbis to tunnel beneath the Dome of the Rock and recover the alleged ark.

12. This remains true even if one should appeal to a text like Rev 11:19: "Then God's temple in heaven was opened, and within his temple was seen the ark of his covenant." One could argue that God transported the ark to heaven before Nebuchadnezzar destroyed the temple. In fact, one late Jewish tradition says the angels of God did take it to heaven. But given the highly symbolic nature of the book of Revelation, it is precarious to insist that the historical ark of the covenant is now in the heavenly throne room. The book of Hebrews portrays the objects of the tabernacle as mere copies of the heavenly realities, just "shadows of the good things that are coming" (Heb 10:1). In short, the NT accords no eschatological function to the historical ark of the covenant.

comprehensive peace between Israel and the Palestinian Authority. Our concern as Christians ought to be first and foremost to act as peacemakers, not enablers of a third temple. Remember, believers now constitute God's spiritual temple, and there is no temple (or need for one) in the new Jerusalem (Rev 21:22). Jeremiah anticipates this eventuality when he says, "It will never enter their minds or be remembered; it will not be missed, nor will another one be made. At that time they will call Jerusalem the Throne of the LORD, and all nations will gather in Jerusalem to honor the name of the LORD" (Jer 3:16–17). In short, Christian "arkeology" is misguided.

The reason for the dramatic turnaround in the fortunes of the people of Israel lies in the brief statement, "No longer will they follow the stubbornness of their evil hearts" (3:17b). The explanation for how this change in attitude comes about is a major contribution of the Book of Consolation. Not to be overlooked in this concluding section is the emphasis upon the unification of Judah and Israel in their ancestral homeland.

Jeremiah 23:3–8: The Remnant and the Righteous King

The second salvation oracle occurring outside the Book of Consolation picks up on the themes of a remnant and the return to the land. The focal point of the passage, however, describes a remarkable, royal figure who accomplishes the seemingly impossible dream: the establishment of a truly just and righteous government and the final salvation and safety of Judah and Israel. Most likely this prophecy should be placed in the latter part of Zedekiah's reign, during the dark days of the Babylonian siege of Jerusalem (see Jer 21:1–2). The contrast between present reality and visionary future couldn't be more stark. The flow of the passage is as follows:

- A remnant regathered from the dispersion (23:3)
- A restoration of responsible government (23:4)
- A righteous king of Davidic descent saves Judah and Israel (23:5–6)

105

Our interest centers on this remarkable prophecy of a Davidic king. Notice the title for this royal figure: "a righteous Branch." This figure of speech goes back to Isaiah of the eighth century BC (Isa 4:2; 11:1). He employed a literary trope that would be reused and adapted by both Jeremiah (Jer 23:5; 33:15) and Zechariah (Zech 3:8; 6:12). The rabbis understood this figure of speech to refer to the promised Messiah.[13] Although no NT author cites it as a messianic text, it was almost certainly so understood by the early Christians. Isaiah uses the expression to refer to a descendant of David from the house of Jesse (Isa 11:1; cf. 1 Sam 16; 17:12, 58; 2 Sam 23:1; Matt 1:6; Acts 13:22; Rom 15:12). Endowed with the sevenfold enabling of the Spirit of Yahweh, this king rules with justice and righteousness (Isa 11:4a). He destroys the wicked (Isa 11:4b) and ushers in a virtual paradise in which harm and violence are forever banished (Isa 11:9). Clearly, the NT picture of the future reign of Jesus fulfills this prophecy of the triumphant kingdom of God on earth (cf. 1 Cor 15:24–28; Col 3:4; 2 Thess 1:5–10; 2:8–10; Rev 20–22; 2 Pet 3:10–14).

One further observation should be made. Jeremiah probably intends his readers to catch the deliberate irony implied by the name of the Davidic scion: "The LORD Our Righteous Savior."[14] Zedekiah's name literally means "my righteousness is Yahweh." The name of the promised Davidic descendant is literally "Yahweh is our righteousness (and savior)." The transposition of key terms signals a dramatic reversal from the grim days of a king who failed to live up to the meaning of his name (Zedekiah) to the glorious days of a king who exceeds in every way the meaning of his name. This is but one of many examples showcasing the literary and theological giftedness of our prophet Jeremiah.

For the sake of completeness, I briefly mention three additional salvation passages that, in the received text, are placed after the Book of Consolation. These passages, for the most part, reiterate themes previously proclaimed. I list each and make a few comments about its contribution.

13. *Tg.* on Jer 23:5.
14. Craigie, *Jeremiah 1–25*, 329.

Jeremiah's Vision of the Future

Jeremiah 46:27–28: Exhortation to Jacob

Sounding very much like passages from Isaiah (e.g., Isa 45), the whole people of Israel, addressed as Jacob, are exhorted not to fear. They are assured that Yahweh is with them through this traumatic episode of destruction and dispersion.[15] This experience is a necessary time of disciplining, a "darkest valley" (Ps 23:4), but it will be tempered ("in due measure") and temporary—they will survive it (v. 28).

Jeremiah 50:4–5: Repentance, Return, and Renewal

This remarkable passage depicts a repentant remnant wending its way on the roads leading to Zion, the ancient city of Jerusalem. Their steps are soaked in tears as they seek Yahweh's favor once again. The emphasis falls upon the determination of the returnees to bind themselves to Yahweh in an eternal covenant (v. 5). This picks up on a major element elaborated in the Book of Consolation.

Jeremiah 50:19–20: A Remnant Returns and Yahweh Removes Their Guilt

This passage has two foci: a return to the rich pasturelands of the ancestral homeland (v. 19) and the removal of the remnant's sins (v. 20). The former describes the returnees as if they were cattle or sheep feeding on the fertile heights of Mt. Carmel and Bashan (the modern Golan Heights) and in the hill country of Ephraim (called the West Bank by Palestinians and Samaria by Israelis) and Gilead (located on the eastern side of the Jordan Valley in the Hashemite Kingdom of Jordan). The second focus depicts divine forgiveness by means of a striking word picture; there is an unsuccessful search for guilt and sin: "none will be found" (v. 20). That's because

---

15. Lundbom emphasizes that the "'I will be with you' promise is bedrock Old Testament theology." *Prophet Like Moses*, 15.

Yahweh has forgiven the repentant remnant. In short, the slate was wiped clean. This is amazing grace.

Jeremiah 50:34; 51:6–10: Settling the Score and Fleeing the Premises

I briefly mention these two texts together even though they are not, strictly speaking, salvation oracles. Rather, they speak into the situation of a people living in a pagan land. How are they to cope? Two points are uppermost. First, they must always remember who Yahweh is. He is their strong deliverer possessing unrivaled power. But he is also a God of justice and a God of compassion: ultimately, he will bring unrest (retribution) upon the Babylonians and provide rest (salvation) for his people.

The second point highlighted by 51:6–9 is a reminder of Yahweh's imminent vengeance upon the arrogant and cruel Babylonian oppressors. The Jewish exiles must be alert to the day of reckoning for the capital city of Babylon. They must make every effort to flee before the siege begins. To remain would result in certain death. The watchword is clear: "Flee from Babylon!" (v. 6). There is every reason to believe they did so. Note that Jesus likewise warned his followers: "When you see Jerusalem being surrounded by armies, you will know that its desolation is near. Then let those who are in Judea flee to the mountains, let those in the city get out, and let those in the country not enter the city. For this is the time of punishment in fulfillment of all that has been written" (Luke 21:20–22). In fact, according to the church historian Eusebius, that is precisely what the believers did prior to the siege of Jerusalem in AD 70.[16]

These two ideas were instrumental in preserving a Jewish remnant to this very day. They are also vital truths that have sustained Christians through the many hard times of oppression and persecution.[17] The reuse of this passage in the Apocalypse of

---

16. *Hist. eccl.* 3.5.3.
17. On this, see further Helyer, *Exploring Jewish Literature*, 57–72, 177.

JEREMIAH'S VISION OF THE FUTURE

John points toward a final showdown between the kingdom of Antichrist and the kingdom of Christ, symbolized by two dramatically opposed cities: Babylon the Great, "the great prostitute" (Rev 18–19), and the new Jerusalem, the glorious bride of Christ (Rev 21). Jeremiah celebrates in anticipation Yahweh's victory over the Babylon of his day (Jer 51:10); John celebrates in anticipation the Lord's victory over the end-time Babylon (Rev 18:20).[18]

I now turn to the Book of Consolation for a more expansive vision of the last days.

BOOK OF CONSOLATION (JER 30-33)

General Comments

We begin by providing an overview of this block of material:

- Jeremiah 30:1—31:26: poetic oracles placed in a period referred to as "the days are coming," "in days to come," and "at that time" (30:3, 24; 31:1). These oracles conclude with a temporal notice informing us that they came to the prophet in a dream: "At this I awoke and looked around. My sleep had been pleasant to me" (31:26).

---

18. John's depiction of Babylon the Great is unmistakably cast in the imagery of first-century AD imperial Rome. "Clearly, the text is not concerned with Babylon now long gone. In this profound suggestive literature, Babylon has resurfaced, now in the form of hated brutalizing Rome. The text has no need to decode or interpret 'Babylon' for its primary readers." Brueggemann, "Texts That Linger," 196. This does not mean that modern interpreters should insist on a literal revival of Rome in the end time. Quite the contrary, the kingdom of Antichrist will incorporate many of the same characteristics and evils as imperial Rome. Michael Brown captures the point: "Because Babylon is given such prominence in the Scriptures—from the tower of Babel in Genesis 11 to these oracles to the book of Daniel—and because it represents the epitome of human pride and world conquest, it becomes a type of all hostile world powers, serving as the ultimate anti-God symbol in Revelation 17:1—19:5. Thus its final demise, prophesied so forcefully here, is representative of the final collapse of all humanly made kingdoms—be they religious or secular—that take the place of God" (*Jeremiah-Ezekiel*, 531).

- Jeremiah 31:27–39: poetic oracles of a similar nature placed in a prose time frame described as "the days are coming" (31:27, 31, 38).

- Jeremiah 32: This prose narrative of Jeremiah's purchase of a piece of property in Anathoth is sandwiched between restoration prophecies. We've already looked at this episode in connection with Jeremiah's symbolic actions. Its significance here in the Book of Consolation is to demonstrate tangibly the prophet's conviction that the restoration oracles will indeed be fulfilled at some unspecified time in the future.

- Jeremiah 33: prose oracles of restoration received while Jeremiah was under house arrest in the courtyard of the guard (33:1).[19] The significance of the temporal setting lies in the fact that we are almost at the end of the line—city and temple are about to be utterly destroyed. Against that grim prospect the restoration oracles stand out in bold relief.

There are any number of suggestions as to how the larger block of material is structurally organized. For example, one might identify separate poems based on the recurrence of the prophetic messenger formula "This is what the LORD says" (30:2, 12, 18; 31:2, 7, 15, 35, 37). But there is no scholarly agreement on this and a wide variety of structural patterns have been proposed.[20] I prefer to approach this section thematically.

Leading Themes

Rescue and Return to the Land

A recurring motif running like a thread throughout is that of Yahweh's rescue and regathering of his exiled people in the ancestral homeland, epitomized in this text: "'I will bring my people Israel and Judah back from captivity and restore them to the land I gave their ancestors to possess,' says the LORD" (30:3). This raises a

---

19. There is one brief poetic passage in 33:15–16.
20. For a survey of options, see Keown and Scalise, *Jeremiah*, 26–52, 86–87.

Jeremiah's Vision of the Future

controversial question. How should we interpret prophetic texts that speak of a return of the Jewish people to their homeland? Are these passages intended as literal or figurative? If not literal, should they be spiritualized as now applying to the church?[21] Another related question concerns the nature of these promises. Are they conditional or unconditional? In other words, is their fulfillment contingent upon certain conditions first being met?

Within conservative Protestant circles, these questions have been differently answered, reflecting a major theological divide. On the one hand, there are those who insist on a more or less literal interpretation, resulting in the conviction that God's ancient people, the Jewish people, will play a vital role in the wrap-up of redemptive history. A literal return of the Jewish people to their ancestral homeland, accompanied at some point by their conversion to Christ, figures prominently in this understanding. This view typically goes under the heading of premillennialism, that is, the notion that Christ will return to earth *before* ("pre-") he establishes his worldwide millennial rule centered in Jerusalem. At the end of this reign there is one last rebellion led by Satan. It is quickly defeated and the devil is forever banished to the lake of fire (Rev 20:7–10). This is followed by the great white throne judgment and the establishment of a new heaven and new earth (Rev 21–22; cf. 1 Cor 15:23–28).[22] Its opposite number—generally, but not always, held by adherents of Reformed theology—interprets the texts under consideration as figurative or spiritual, that is, they apply now to the church and not to the Jewish people. Christ is reigning spiritually over his people from his throne in heaven, whether they are still alive on earth (the so-called church militant) or whether they have died and reign with Christ in his presence (the so-called

---

21. Dearman, for example, understands their fulfillment within the church, composed of believing Jews and Gentiles (*Jeremiah and Lamentations*, 267–71).

22. The word *millennium* designates a period of one thousand years. This term occurs five times in Rev 20:1–6. Premillennialists generally relate this period to the messianic age of peace in which justice and righteousness reign as depicted in the OT prophets (e.g., Isa 2:1–5; 11:1–16; 35; Amos 9:11–15; Micah 5:1–15, et al.).

church triumphant). The return of Christ does not include a literal reign on the earth, whether for a thousand years or some indefinite period of time. For this reason it is often referred to as amillennialism.[23] A variant is postmillennialism, in which the millennium is a figurative expression for the triumph *in history* of the kingdom of Christ on earth. This millennial reign (understood as lasting a long time but not necessarily one thousand years) is followed by a brief rebellion that is quelled by Christ's Second Advent, the final judgment, and the eternal state. My comments oversimplify a complex issue but, I hope, are sufficient to understand the primary options.[24]

Here is my take on this highly debated issue. I hold that the OT prophecies about the regathering and return to the land should be taken literally. This is not to deny that NT writers do indeed spiritualize many aspects of OT teaching. As just one example, the new people of God, the church of Jesus Christ consisting of both Jew and Gentile, is clearly likened to a new temple and its members are styled as priests (1 Cor 3:16; 6:19–20; Eph 2:14–22; 1 Pet 2:4–10). The terminology and imagery of the OT people of God are repeatedly reapplied to the NT people of God and numerous examples could be brought forward to illustrate. But this adaptation of OT vocabulary does not require a wholesale spiritualizing of the many concrete prophecies about a return of the Jewish people to the land. The attempt to spiritualize the notions of exile, regathering, and return to the land in terms of the NT church stretches language to the breaking point. Paul and John, for instance, still anticipate that the Jewish people will return to their native olive tree and be regrafted into the people of God (Rom

---

23. The word *amillenial*, meaning literally "no millennium," is not really the best word to describe this view, inasmuch as adherents understand the expression to refer to the actual, present reign of Christ over the church, a period of time now exceeding two thousand years. In other words, the length of time should not be taken literally but the reality behind it should. Probably a term like "realized kingdom" or "present kingdom" better captures the position of adherents.

24. For a fuller discussion of millennial views, see Clouse, *Meaning of the Millennium*, and Bock, *Three Views on the Millennium*.

Jeremiah's Vision of the Future

11:11–36; Rev 7:4–8; 14:1–5). Jeremiah's repeated prophecies about the irrevocable nature of God's promise to restore Israel as a nation in their homeland (Jer 31:17; 32:37–41; 33:19–26) chimes in with Paul's certainty about their conversion (Rom 11:29). How can one justify separating the certainty of their future conversion from the certainty of their literal restoration in the land?

There is, however, another troublesome matter that must be addressed. Did not the Jewish people return from exile and rebuild their land and reestablish political autonomy in it? The answer, of course, is yes. There was a remarkable return of a remnant and an equally remarkable establishment of a second commonwealth. This story is narrated in Ezra and Nehemiah and continued in 1 and 2 Maccabees as well as in the Jewish historian Josephus. One may recall the heroic deeds of the Maccabees as they are popularly known. The Hasmonean dynasty lasted from about 142 BC to 63 BC.[25] This approximately one-hundred-year period witnessed the rise of Jewish autonomy and power on a par with the golden age of David and Solomon. Unfortunately, the Hasmonean dynasty succumbed to internecine conflict and the intervention of Roman imperial ambitions. Thus during the ministry of Jesus and his apostles, Judea was a Roman province under a Roman-appointed governor. However, just as Jesus prophesied, even this state of affairs would come to a disastrous end (Matt 24; par. Mark 13; Luke 21). In AD 66 the Jews rose up in revolt and sought to throw off the shackles of Roman control. This attempt ended in the catastrophic destruction of many Jewish cities, including Jerusalem and its glorious temple, which ironically occurred on the same calendar day as the destruction of the First Temple. Many perished or were enslaved, others fled to neighboring countries for refuge, and some survivors remained in the land, eking out a meager existence

---

25. The Hasmonean family included a father, Mattathias, and his five sons, John, Simon, Judas, Eleazar, and Jonathan. Judas was nicknamed Maccabeus, meaning "the hammerer." This moniker was later applied to the dynasty. See Helyer, *Exploring Jewish Literature*, 113–17, for a brief overview of this time period.

under Roman authority. The large majority of Jews now lived in Diaspora.[26]

In the latter part of the nineteenth century, a remarkable chain of events began unfolding. A small trickle of Jews began to return to their ancient homeland and a movement to reestablish a Jewish state arose, known as Zionism. Against all odds, this movement achieved what seemed an impossible dream. In May 1948 a Jewish state was proclaimed by David Ben-Gurion, Israel's first prime minister, in Tel Aviv. We are now seventy years into what could be called the Third Commonwealth. The State of Israel is the most powerful military power in the region and has the support of the world's greatest superpower, the United State of America. Where this story goes from here only the Lord of history knows. One thing is certain: the Israelis vow that the holocaust will never happen again. The spirit of the Maccabees has revived. But not to be overlooked are the amazing innovations pioneered by Israelis, especially in the fields of agriculture, computer technology, and medicine. The humanitarian contributions of this very small country are out of all proportion to their numbers. The promise to Abraham still holds true: "All the peoples on earth will be blessed through you" (Gen 12:3b). God is not yet finished with his old covenant people.

Jeremiah prophesied that seventy years after the destruction and deportation of leading citizens, Yahweh would regather his exiles in the land of Israel (Jer 25:12–14; 29:10–14). As narrated above, a remnant did return and that eventually led to an autonomous, powerful Jewish state. But as also rehearsed, the Second Commonwealth was finally shattered by the Romans. The problem is obvious: how do we reconcile that with the divine promise of a deliverance and return that is perpetual (Jer 30:10; 31:11–12; 35–37; 33:25–26)? How do we reconcile the prophecy of the rebuilding of the city (Jer 31:38–40a) and the divine promise that

26. This term refers to the dispersion of Jews after the Babylonian Exile, specifically, the places where they lived. In modern times, until just recently, the single largest community of Jews lived in the United States. Significantly, this changed as we moved into the twenty-first century; today, more Jews live in Israel than in the United States.

Jeremiah's Vision of the Future

"the city will never again be uprooted or demolished" (Jer 31:40b) with historical reality? Clearly, the city was demolished in AD 70 and again in AD 135. As a matter of fact, Jerusalem was sacked many times thereafter.[27]

I think the answer lies in the perspective from which one should view the prophecies of return. The scope of the return, the scale of the return, and the remarkable rebirth connected with the return did not happen in the postexilic period.[28] The prophecies of return are placed in "the last days." But the last days did not begin until the Day of Pentecost when Peter announced that they had begun: "In these last days" (Acts 2:17; cf. Heb 1:2).[29] From that perspective, the modern return of Jews to the land of Israel takes on added significance. In short, we may be witnessing the first stages of a return that culminates in the conversion of the Jewish people and the return of their Jewish messiah, Jesus of Nazareth (Rom 11:25–27). I can't be certain of this, but I think it merits careful consideration. If this interpretation is right, we may well be living in momentous times. Does this mean we should reorient our priorities and become ardent Zionists? I think not. Our marching orders as Christians are clear. We must beware of being hijacked by other agendas. Taking sides in the Israeli-Palestinian dispute is not our calling. As argued above, we are God's spiritual temple and whatever happens in regard to a putative third temple is not our primary concern. So long as the Great Commission remains unfulfilled, we must stay on task. Our calling as Christians centers on a ministry of reconciliation in Christ (2 Cor 5:14–21). Worth noting in this regard is a new reality: we are being assisted by some unexpected allies in proclaiming the good news. A growing remnant of Jewish believers are discovering their Jewish messiah. Messianic Jews in their ancestral homeland are presently sowing the seeds

---

27. Arguably, the most horrific act in connection with the sieges of Jerusalem occurred when, in 1099, the Crusaders took the city from the Muslims. Jews who survived the onslaught were herded into a synagogue and burned alive. This was the nadir of a terribly misguided venture.

28. So Dearman, *Jeremiah and Lamentations*, 267–71.

29. For a similar approach, see Dearman, *Jeremiah and Lamentations*.

of a future harvest of Jewish believers committed to Jesus Christ (cf. Rom 11:12, 15, 25–27). And "wonder of wonders, miracle of miracles," slowly but surely, reconciliation is taking place between Israeli and Palestinian Christians. "Oh, the depth of the riches of the wisdom and knowledge of God!" (Rom 11:33). "To him be the glory forever! Amen" (11:36).

Repentance and Rebirth

Even more remarkable than the return to the homeland is the subsequent repentance and rebirth of the Jewish people, an event still largely unfulfilled, as discussed above. The Book of Consolation first introduces this momentous event in 30:9: "Instead, they will serve the LORD their God and David their king, whom I will raise up for them." What Jeremiah's preaching could not bring about now happens. "I will restore you to health and heal your wounds" (30:17). The grand conclusion of this remarkable rebirth is the goal of redemptive history: "So you will be my people, and I will be your God" (30:22; cf. Rev 21:3). Note that this occurs after an undefined period of punishment for their sins (30:10–16).

The text makes clear that the restoration to spiritual health is not even remotely possible by means of self-help or human help (vv. 13–14). It is an act of sheer grace. God himself works in their hearts to effect this transformation. So, why didn't he do this sooner? The only answer to this question comes in 30:24: "The fierce anger of the LORD will not turn back until he fully accomplishes the purposes of his heart. In days to come you will understand this." In other words, God has a plan that is unfolding in accordance with his will. This reminds us of Paul's words to the Ephesians: "He made known to us the mystery of his will according to his good pleasure, which he purposed in Christ, to be put into effect when the times reach their fulfillment—to bring unity to all things in heaven and on earth under Christ" (Eph 1:9–10). In short, many things remain mysteriously beyond our understanding. Rather than chafe at not having the answer to all our whys, we need to be content with what we do know: "The secret things belong to the LORD our God, but the things revealed belong to us and to our children forever, that we may follow all the word of this law" (Deut 29:29).[30]

But is there a condition that the remnant must first meet before this occurs? One must carefully nuance the answer. According to Jeremiah, there must be a free response to the prior initiative of God's grace. Thus in a remarkable passage the prophet gives voice to the repentant remnant. "I have surely heard Ephraim's moaning: 'You have disciplined me like an unruly calf, and I have been disciplined. Restore me, and I will return, because you are the LORD my God. After I strayed, I repented: after I came to understand, I beat my breast, I was ashamed and humiliated because I bore the disgrace of my youth'" (31:18–19). God's grace is not diminished by the corollary of a genuinely free response to this grace.[31]

What can confidently be affirmed by all believers is God's unfailing love. Several passages highlight this truth: "I have loved you with an everlasting love; I have drawn you with unfailing kindness" (31:3). This love is likened to that of a father: "I will lead them beside streams of water . . . because I am Israel's father, and Ephraim is my firstborn son" (31:9c). The intensity of God's love for Israel is nowhere more powerfully expressed than in 31:20: "'Is not Ephraim my dear son, the child in whom I delight? Though I often speak against him, I still remember him. Therefore my heart yearns for him; I have great compassion for him,' declares the LORD."

---

30. Philip Yancey captures well the point I'm trying to make: "God had answered Job's questions with more questions, as if to say the truths of existence lie far beyond the range of our comprehension" (*Soul Survivor*, 53).

31. I touch here on the highly divisive topic of God's sovereignty and human freedom. My view is slanted toward what is commonly called Arminianism. For a scholarly statement of this position from an evangelical perspective, see Olson, *Arminian Theology*, and Walls and Dongell, *Why I Am Not a Calvinist*.

THE LIFE AND WITNESS OF JEREMIAH

New Covenant

This brings me to the central idea lying at the heart of the Book of Consolation. The return, restoration, and rebirth of the people of Israel take place on the basis of a new covenant between God and his people. Covenants regulate the relationship between God and his people in all times and places. The covenant with Noah (Gen 9) is followed by the covenant with Abraham and his descendants (Gen 12; 15; 17). This is followed by the all-important Sinai covenant with Israel (Exod 19–24). This covenant was still in force during Jeremiah's day, although, as he repeatedly warned his listeners, the people had violated it by their persistent disobedience and rebellion. The question was, what does Yahweh intend to do about it? Jeremiah rails about the consequences of noncompliance staring Judah in the face. The curses for covenant violation (Lev 26:14–46; Deut 28:15–68) culminate in expulsion from the land, a punishment hanging over their heads like a sword of Damocles. Jeremiah lived to see the execution of this ultimate sanction against God's people. But he also proclaimed something truly amazing. Yahweh was going to initiate a new covenant with his people. This new covenant would be a quantum leap forward in terms of its benefits and effectiveness. This calls for closer examination.

The seven poems of restoration in Jeremiah 30:1—31:25 (identified by the messenger formula "This is what the LORD says") conclude with the narrative framework: "At this I awoke and looked around. My sleep had been pleasant to me" (31:26). This is the only recorded instance during Jeremiah's long ministry when he experienced pleasure. His tortured soul found rest in this sure word of a loving and restoring God. This reminds us of John's glowing description of the new heaven and new earth in Revelation 21:4: "There will be no more death or mourning or crying or pain, for the old order of things has passed away." Following his dream vision, Jeremiah receives another vision of the coming days. Once again the theme is return and restoration. Significantly, however, the theme is couched in agricultural terminology recalling the formulation of Jeremiah's original call to be a prophet: "I will

JEREMIAH'S VISION OF THE FUTURE

plant the kingdoms of Israel and Judah with the offspring of people and of animals" (31:27). Then, in an unmistakable allusion to his call, we hear these words: "Just as I watched over them to uproot and tear down, and to overthrow, destroy and bring disaster, so I will watch over them to build and to plant..." (31:28; cf. 1:10).

This is followed by a correction of traditional opinion. We've already drawn attention to Jeremiah's propensity to overturn cherished but mistaken views, as in the temple sermon. In this instance, it was widely accepted that children were punished for the sins of their parents and ancestors, a notion thought to be enshrined even in the Ten Commandments (Exod 20:5-6). A proverbial saying expressed this sentiment: "The parents have eaten sour grapes, and the children's teeth are set on edge" (31:29). But as Jeremiah insists, in the days to come, this proverb will no longer be quoted. The reason is clearly stated: each individual will be held accountable for his or her own sins. In fact, Exodus 20:5-6 doesn't teach that children are punished for the individual sins of their parents; rather, they are subject to the lingering *consequences and effects* of parental sins. This is an important distinction that must be maintained.[32] Furthermore, Deuteronomy 24:16 explicitly forbids punishing children for the sins of their fathers. The point is that Jeremiah's generation hid behind this proverb in order to shift the blame for their calamities onto their parents and ancestors, thereby dodging their own responsibility. This fostered a fatalistic approach to life akin to the notion of *que sera sera* (whatever will be, will be). It should be noted that Jeremiah's contemporary, Ezekiel, who ministered in the refugee camps along the Kebar River (in modern Iraq), confronted the same fatalistic outlook (Ezek 18).

Both prophets indicate that one of the significant changes in the new covenant is the renewed emphasis upon individual responsibility. This notion is so embedded in Western, modern

---

32. Illustrated by the account of David's sin with Bathsheba. His family suffered the consequences of his sin and its aftermath (2 Sam 12-18). Many modern examples could be cited, such as drug addiction and criminal activity in which children, unfortunately, suffer the consequences of their parents' transgressions.

The Life and Witness of Jeremiah

culture we tend to ignore how important it is. In fact, modern jurisprudence is based upon this principle.

The central text on the new covenant is introduced by the familiar eschatological phrase "the days are coming" (31:31). When redemptive history enters its climactic phase, Yahweh establishes a new covenant with his people Israel and Judah. Jeremiah emphasizes its dissimilarity to the first covenant at Mt. Sinai. The problem with the first covenant lay in the failure of Israel and Judah to keep it: "they broke my covenant" (v. 32). The feature of the new covenant that prevents a similar breakdown is now spelled out: "I will put my law in their minds and write it on their hearts" (v. 33). In other words, Yahweh changes the hearts of the covenant partners so that they willingly obey the obligations of the new covenant.[33] Furthermore, all the new covenant people truly know the Lord to such an extent that teaching its contents is no longer necessary. This internal fix results in the goal of redemptive history being realized, namely, "I will be their God, and they will be my people" (v. 33b) and "I will forgive their wickedness and remember their sins no more" (v. 34). This new state of affairs can only be realized by a radical change of heart, the equivalent of a new birth.[34] Although Jeremiah does not employ new-birth terminology, only in light of it can one make sense of what actually happens. Jeremiah's contemporary, Ezekiel, makes explicit what is implicit in Jeremiah's imagery. "I will sprinkle clean water on you, and you will be clean; I will cleanse you from all your impurities and from all your idols. I will give you a new heart and put a new spirit in you; I will remove from you your heart of stone and give you a heart of flesh. I will put my Spirit in you and move you to follow my decrees and be careful to keep my laws" (Ezek 36:25–27). Note that Ezekiel clearly locates this amazing new birth *after* the regathering from exile (Ezek 36:24).

---

33. "At least sixty-six times the word 'heart' is found in the Book of Jeremiah, for he is preeminently the prophet of the heart." Wiersbe, *Be Decisive*, 12.

34. "Our modern age is a pushover for the shallow and the shortcut. We want to change everything except the human heart." Hamilton, *Thunder of Bare Feet*, 69.

It goes without saying how crucial this concept is for NT theology. John's Gospel preserves a saying of Jesus that makes this striking point: "Very truly I tell you, no one can enter the kingdom of God without being born of water and the Spirit" (John 3:5). The new birth (1 Pet 1:3) and its equivalent in Paul, "raised to new life" (Eph 2:4–6), are central to the good news. Jeremiah and Ezekiel prophesied its reality hundreds of years before it is proclaimed by Jesus and his apostles. There can be little doubt that Jesus had the new covenant of Jeremiah and Ezekiel in mind when he shared the Last Supper with his apostles. Luke's Gospel preserves this saying of Jesus: "This cup is the new covenant in my blood, which is poured out for you" (Luke 22:20; cf. Matt 26:28–29). The eighth chapter of Hebrews, in which the author quotes extensively from Jeremiah 31, contains the most extensive elaboration of this important theological truth. The writer concludes his long quotation by observing, "By calling this covenant 'new,' he has made the first one obsolete; and what is obsolete and outdated will soon disappear" (Heb 8:13).

New Covenant Champion

Finally, we notice that once again a central figure appears in this closing drama. It is that previously mentioned (23:5–6) righteous Branch from David's line who both saves and secures the people of Israel and Judah (33:15). His appearance in the story occurs in the coming days, that is, the eschatological end time. The correspondence with the NT witness concerning Jesus the Messiah has already been rehearsed. I add this observation on the narrative passage following the poem (vv. 15–16). Here we have the divine promise that "David will never fail to have a man sit on the throne of the house of Israel, nor will the Levitical priests ever fail to have a man to stand before me continually to offer burnt offerings, to burn grain offerings and to present sacrifice" (31:17–18). The historical facts are clear: Zedekiah was the last Jewish king to reign over Judah, although his reign was that of a vassal seeking vainly to free his little kingdom from the overlordship of Babylon and its king, Nebuchadnezzar. The Hasmoneans were not descendants of David, nor was the later Herodian dynasty. In short, no other Davidic Jewish king has literally reigned over the Jewish people from Zedekiah's time till the present. Furthermore, the Levitical priesthood ceased in AD 70 and has never been reconstituted.[35]

That begs a question: When, if ever, will this divine oracle be fulfilled? The NT provides the answer. Jesus of Nazareth, KING OF KINGS AND LORD OF LORDS (Rev 19:16; cf. Acts 2:33), is now reigning over the new people of God, comprised of both Jews and Gentiles, from his heavenly throne at the right hand of God the Father. He is an eternal being and his reign is likewise eternal (Eph 2:6; Phil 2:9–11; Col 3:1), but he is also a human being from the house of David as the NT amply testifies (Matt 1:1–16; Luke 3:32; Rom 1:3; 2 Tim 2:8). Therefore, he alone fulfills the divine promise. Furthermore, the Levitical priesthood under the new covenant has been replaced by the superior priesthood of Melchizedek. As the great high priest, Jesus makes everlasting intercession for his people and his once-for-all-sacrifice is sufficient for all time. This is the message of Hebrews (Heb 4:14—10:22). As can be seen, this answer involves the recognition of both literal and spiritual elements in the fulfillment of Jeremiah's prophecy. In my opinion, this provides a coherent, satisfying position.

CONCLUSION

This chapter has covered a large topic in a short space and raised a number of debated questions. I have sought to set forth my understanding of the basic issues and leave it to the reader to make his or her own determination as to their correctness. On this point, however, virtually all interpreters agree: the Book of Consolation plays an important role as a counterbalance in the book as a whole. Most of Jeremiah's prophecies are judgment oracles of gloom and

---

35. The Temple Institute, composed of Orthodox Jews, is making plans for the building of the third temple and resumption of the Levitical sacrifices. This group, however, does not speak for the Israeli government, nor does it represent the majority view of Israelis.

doom. Here in this section we have some blessed relief and the sun comes out. God's last word to Israel and Judah through his messenger Jeremiah is a word of consolation and hope.[36] That hope shines forth in glorious splendor in the NT and becomes reality in and through Jesus Christ, "The LORD our Righteous Savior" (Jer 23:6; cf. 1 Cor 1:30; 2 Cor 5:21).

---

36. "Hope is the primary prophetic idiom not because of the general dynamic of history or because of the signs of the times but because the prophet speaks to a people who, willy-nilly, are God's people. Hope is what this community must do because it is God's community invited to be in God's pilgrimage." Brueggemann, *Prophetic Imagination*, 66.

7

Epilogue

The time spent researching and writing on the life and witness of Jeremiah opened up new vistas for me. Specifically, Jeremiah's relevance for issues of faith and politics refocused my attention on a challenging aspect of Christian living. Reflecting on Jeremiah's powerful sermon against a spiritually bankrupt nationalism, I sense "a clear and present danger" lurking in every generation, but especially our own, in which Christian nationalism threatens to sidetrack us from our primary task. Jeremiah believed what Jesus later proclaimed: "My kingdom is not of this world. If it were, my servants would fight to prevent my arrest by the Jewish leaders. But now my kingdom is from another place" (John 18:36).[1] We who are followers of Jesus need to pause and ask ourselves, What is our agenda and what should it be?

The degree of Jeremiah's sufferings in being a faithful spokesperson of Yahweh had not fully dawned on me prior to writing this book. Jeremiah was a sensitive man who sought affirmation. I identify with him in this regard. Virtually all of us crave strokes. I'm not as courageous as Jeremiah. I would be terrified to take public stances in the face of bitter opposition. I want people to like me and say nice things about me. So did Jeremiah. The question I

---

1. See also Matt 6:33.

struggle with is, Where do I draw a line in the sand? When do I say, "This goes too far"? When do I speak out, to my own discomfort? Engaging Jeremiah's preaching compelled me to speak my mind on a very divisive issue. Some readers will sharply disagree with my criticism of Christian nationalism. In their view, I'm misguided. For my part, I sincerely believe I'm on the right track. In the next breath, however, I acknowledge that my interpretation and application of Scripture is neither inspired nor infallible. As the Apostle Paul reminds us, we "see only a reflection as in a mirror . . . and know in part" (1 Cor 13:12). Thankfully, the Spirit of God has not compelled me, like Jeremiah, to take on my coreligionists in live public forums! My foray is much less daunting, a book with a limited audience. I do hope, however, that some readers will reconsider or even change their position as a result of hearing afresh the message of Jeremiah.

Jeremiah's dogged determination to "hang in there" in spite of unrelenting opposition has inspired and motivated me. In that regard, he serves as a fellow traveler for those facing their hour of trial. Persecution for the name of Christ is a global reality. Many unknown and unsung heroes of the faith are undergoing a baptism by fire. May the Lord who rescued Jeremiah from the pit be their strong deliverer!

Studying Jeremiah, I have been reminded that all saints are flawed, even heroes like Jeremiah.[2] His outbursts against Yahweh allow me to identify with him. He had his issues, and so do I. This is not to justify my flaws and sins, but to be reminded that the process of becoming holy is never a straight line or a constantly ascending curve. There are many zigs and zags with precipitous dips along the way. Reliving Jeremiah's life has helped me become more sympathetic to the perceived flaws and shortcomings of fellow believers, and, I hope, more compassionate toward them because of my own.

That brings me to a concluding observation: reading Jeremiah has reaffirmed my hope for the future. Yahweh's unshakeable commitment to restore Israel lies at the heart of the new covenant. As

---

2. A point eloquently chronicled in Yancey, *Soul Survivor*.

The Life and Witness of Jeremiah

the NT proclaims, that restoration promise undergoes tremendous development, enlarging its scope to nothing short of all creation (Col 1:20; 2 Pet 3: 10–13; Rev 21:5). May this conviction sustain all believers during the arduous climb to the summit of the heavenly Mt. Zion.[3] I have another hope. When the new Jerusalem finally arrives in all its glory and splendor, I want to interview some of my theological heroes in Scripture—I have a lot of questions for them. When I get an opportunity to meet Jeremiah, I plan to give him a big hug. I'm hoping this will be a pleasant experience for him (Jer 31:26). Thanks, Jeremiah, for staying the course!

---

3. For the metaphor of the Christian life as a mountain climb, see my comments in *Mountaintop Theology*, 147–48. For a powerful use of mountain climbing imagery during the civil rights movement, see Martin Luther King Jr., "I Have a Dream."

Appendix

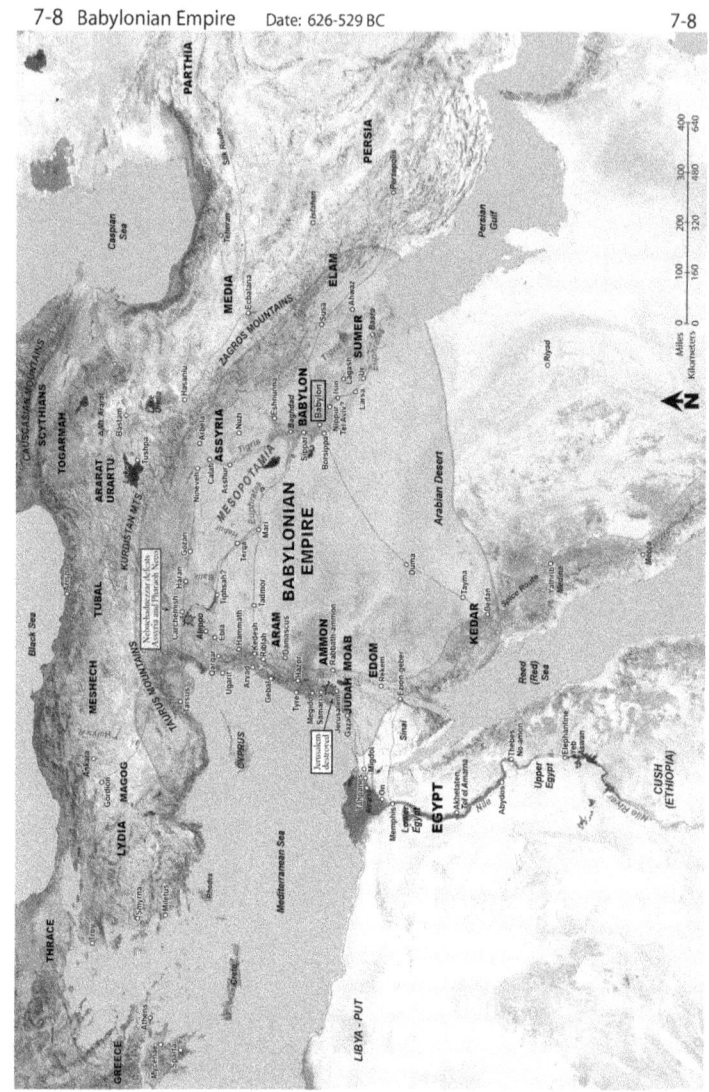

Satellite Bible Atlas
Historical Geography of the Bible
@2008, 2011 by William Schlegel. All rights reserved.
Used by permission of the author

7-9 The Fall of Jerusalem: Babylonian Conquest Date: 586 BC 7-9

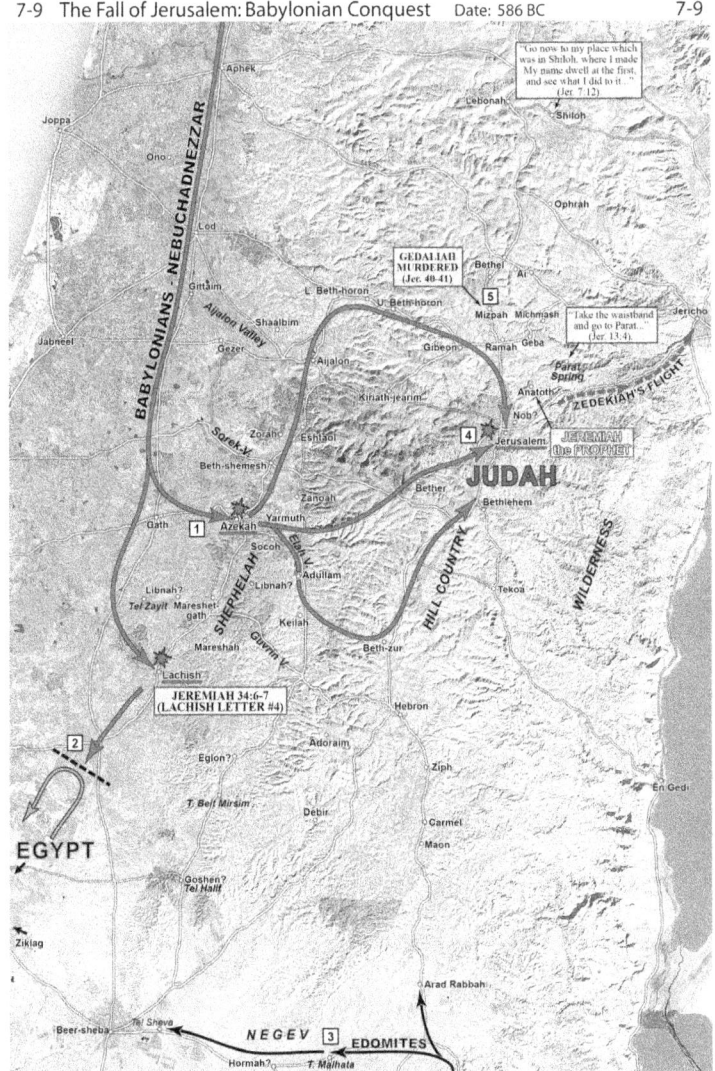

Satellite Bible Atlas
Historical Geography of the Bible
@2008, 2011 by William Schlegel. All rights reserved.
Used by permission of the author

Bibliography

Aharoni, Y. "Excavations at Ramat Rahel, 1954: Preliminary Report." *IEJ* 6 (1956) 102–11, 137–57.
Barkay, Gabriel. "Ramat Rahel." In *NEAEHL* 4:1479–84.
———. "Royal Palace, Royal Portrait?" *BAR* 32 (2006) 34–44.
Barton, David. *America's Godly Heritage*. Aledo, TX: WallBuilders, 2009.
———. *The Jefferson Lies: Exposing the Myths You've Always Believed about Thomas Jefferson*. Nashville: Nelson, 2012.
Bock, Darrell L., ed. *Three Views on the Millennium and Beyond*. Grand Rapids: Zondervan, 1999.
The Book of Common Prayer and Administration of the Sacraments and Other Rites and Ceremonies of the Church. New York: Church Hymnal, 1977.
Boyd, Gregory A. *The Myth of a Christian Nation: How the Quesst for Political Power Is Destroying the Church*. Grand Rapids: Zondervan, 2005.
———. "Racism: Why Whites Have Trouble 'Getting It.'" *Reknew. org*, January 25, 2007. https://reknew.org/2007/01/racism-why-whites-have-trouble-getting-it-1-25-07/.
Brown, Michael L. *Jeremiah–Ezekiel*. EBC 7. Grand Rapids: Zondervan, 2010.
Brueggemann, Walter. *The Prophetic Imagination*. 2nd ed. Minneapolis: Fortress, 2001.
———. "Texts That Linger, Words That Explode." *Theology Today* 54 (1997) 180–99.
———. *To Pluck Up, to Tear Down: A Commentary on the Book of Jeremiah 1–25*. International Theological Commentary. Grand Rapids: Eerdmans, 1988.
Clouse, Robert G., ed. *The Meaning of the Millennium: Four Views*. Downers Grove: InterVarsity, 1977.
Craigie, Peter C. *Jeremiah 1–25*. Word Biblical Commentary 26. Dallas: Word, 1991.
Daly, Jim. "The Importance of Listening in Today's Evangelicalism." In *Still Evangelical? Insiders Reconsider Political, Social, and Theological Meaning*, edited by Mark Labberton, 173–83. Downers Grove: InterVarsity, 2018.

Bibliography

Dearman, J. Andrew. *Jeremiah and Lamentations*. NIVAC. Grand Rapids: Zondervan, 2002.
DeYoung, Curtiss Paul, et al. *United by Faith: The Multicultural Congregation as an Answer to the Problem of Race*. New York: Oxford University Press, 2003.
Emerson, Michael O., and Christian Smith. *Divided by Faith: Evangelical Religion and the Problem of Race in America*. New York: Oxford University Press, 2000.
Fea, John. *Believe Me: The Evangelical Road to Donald Trump*. Grand Rapids: Eerdmans, 2018.
———. *Was America Founded as a Christian Nation? A Historical Introduction*. Rev. ed. Louisville: Westminster John Knox. 2016.
Ford, Michael. *Wounded Prophet: A Portrait of Henri J. M. Nouwen*. New York: Doubleday, 1999.
Foster, Benjamin. "The Babylonian Theodicy." In *COS* 1:492–95.
Green, William Scott. "False Messiahs." In *The Encyclopedia of Judaism*, edited by Jacob Neusner et al., 2:883–88. Leiden: Brill, 2000.
Hamilton, J. Wallace. *The Thunder of Bare Feet*. Westwood, NJ: Revell, 1964.
Hays, Richard B. *The Moral Vision of the New Testament: Community, Cross, New Creation; A Contemporary Introduction to New Testament Ethics*. San Francisco: HarperSanFrancisco, 1996.
Helyer, Larry. *Exploring Jewish Literature of the Second Temple Period*. Downers Grove: InterVarsity, 2002.
———. "The Hasmoneans and the Hasmonean Era." In *The World of the New Testament: Social, Cultural, and Historical Contexts*, edited by Joel B. Green and Lee Martin McDonald, 38–53. Grand Rapids: Baker, 2013.
———. *The Life and Witness of Peter*. Downers Grove: InterVarsity, 2012.
———. *Mountaintop Theology: Panoramic Perspectives of Redemptive History*. Eugene, OR: Cascade, 2016.
———. *Yesterday, Today, and Forever: The Continuing Relevance of the Old Testament*. Rev. ed. Salem, WI: Sheffield, 2002.
Hicks, R. Lansing. "*Delet* and *megillah*: A Fresh Approach to Jer XXXVI." *VT* 33 (1983) 46–66.
Holladay, William Lee. *Jeremiah: A Commentary on the Book of the Prophet Jeremiah (Chapters 1–25)*. Hermeneia. Philadelphia: Fortress, 1986.
———. *Jeremiah 2: A Commentary on the Book of the Prophet Jeremiah (Chapters 26–52)*. Hermeneia. Philadelphia: Fortress, 1990.
———. *Jeremiah: Spokesman Out of Time*. New York: Pilgrim, 1974.
House, Paul R. "Plot, Prophecy and Jeremiah." *JETS* 36 (1993) 297–306.
Keown, Gerald L., and Pamela J. Scalise. *Jeremiah 26–52*. Word Biblical Commentary 27. Dallas: Word, 1995.
Labberton, Mark. "Political Dealing: The Crisis of Evangelicalism." Speech given at a private meeting of evangelical leaders held at Wheaton College, Chicago, IL, April 16, 2018. https://www.fuller.edu/posts/political-dealing-the-crisis-of-evangelicalism/.

Bibliography

Labberton, Mark, ed. *Still Evangelical? Insiders Reconsider Political, Social, and Theological Meaning.* Downers Grove: InterVarsity, 2018.

LaHaye, Tim. *Faith of Our Founding Fathers.* Green Forest, AR: Master Books, 1994.

Larsen, Josh. "Are Evangelicals in Denial about Racism?" *Think Christian*, May 10, 2016. https://thinkchristian.reframemedia.com/are-evangelicals-in-denial-about-racism?

Latourette, Kenneth Scott. *A History of Christianity.* New York: Harper, 1953.

Lundbom, Jack R. *Jeremiah: A Prophet Like Moses.* Eugene, OR: Cascade, 2015.

———. *Jeremiah 1–20.* AB 21A. New York: Doubleday, 1999.

———. *Jeremiah 21–36.* AB 21B. New York: Doubleday, 2001.

———. *Jeremiah 37–52.* AB 21C. New York: Doubleday, 2004.

MacLean, H. B. "Josiah." In *IBD* 2:999.

Marshall, Peter, and David Manuel. *The Light and the Glory.* Old Tappan, NJ: Revell, 1977.

Moore, J. L. "Race in Evangelical America." *Christian Reflection: A Series in Faith and Ethics* (2010) 82–86.

Morgan, G. Campbell. *Studies in the Prophecy of Jeremiah.* Westbrook, NJ: Revell, 1960.

New Analytical Bible and Dictionary of the Bible. Chicago: Dickson, 1950.

Olmstead, Clifton E. *History of Religion in the United States.* Englewood Cliffs, NJ: Prentice-Hall, 1960.

Olson, Roger E. *Arminian Theology: Myths and Reality.* Downers Grove: InterVarsity, 2006.

Overholt, Thomas W. *The Threat of Falsehood: A Study in the Theology of the Book of Jeremiah.* Studies in Biblical Theology, Second Series, 16. Naperville, IL: A. R. Allenson, 1970.

Patterson, Richard D. "Of Bookends, Hinges, and Hooks: Literary Clues to the Arrangement of Jeremiah's Prophecies." *WTJ* 51 (1989) 109–31.

Petersen, William J. *Jeremiah: The Prophet Who Wouldn't Quit.* Wheaton, IL: Victor, 1984.

Peterson, Eugene H. *Run with the Horses: The Quest for Life at Its Best.* 2nd ed. Downers Grove, IL: IVP, 2009.

Robertson, Pat. *America's Dates with Destiny.* Nashville: Nelson, 1986.

Schneider, Tsvi. "Six Biblical Signatures: Seals and Seal Impressions of Six Biblical Personages Recovered." *BAR* 17 (1991) 26–33.

Sider, Ronald. "Why I Am Voting for Hillary Clinton." *Christianity Today*, October 2016, 54.

Smietana, Bob. "Prosperity Gospel Taught to 4 in 10 Evangelical Churchgoers." *Christianity Today*, July 31, 2018. https://www.christianitytoday.com/news/2018/july/prosperity-gospel-survey-churchgoers-prosper-tithe-blessing.html.

Smith, Ralph L. "The Book of Jeremiah." *Southwestern Journal of Theology* 4 (1961). http://preachingsource.com/journal/the-book-of-jeremiah/.

BIBLIOGRAPHY

Walls, Jerry L., and Joseph R. Dongell. *Why I Am Not a Calvinist.* Downers Grove: InterVarsity, 2004.
Waltke, Bruce. *An Old Testament Theology.* Grand Rapids: Zondervan, 2007.
Wiersbe, Warren W. *Be Decisive.* Wheaton, IL: Victor, 1995.
Wilsey, John D. *American Exceptionalism and Civil Religion: Reassessing the History of an Idea.* Downers Grove: InterVarsity Academic, 2015.
Winthrop, John. "A Modell of Christian Charity." In *God's New Israel: Religious Interpretations of American Destiny*, edited by Conrad Cherry, 37–41. Rev. ed. Chapel Hill: University of North Carolina Press, 1998.
Yancey, Philip. *Soul Survivor: How Thirteen Unlikely Mentors Helped My Faith Survive the Church.* Colorado Springs: Galilee/WaterBrook, 2003.

Index

Abiathar, 2
Abraham
  covenant, 118
  promises to, 114
  protestations, 76
addressees of prophecies, 100
Adonijah, 2
Ahijah, 41
Ahikam, 28–29, 29n14
Ain Fara (spring), 43
amillenialism, 112, 112n23
Ammon, 51, 100–101
Amos, 6n14, 16–17, 24, 59–60
Anathoth, 2, 2n4, 53–54, 79–80, 110
Anna, 60
antiphonal hymn, 21
antisocial behavior of Jeremiah, 45–46, 88–89
apostasy, 9–10n21
apostles, 18
apostolic teachings, 69–71
ark of the covenant, 103–4, 104nn11–12
Asaph, 81
Ashurbanipal, 3
Assyria, 3, 7–8, 11, 43

Baal, 50, 61
Babylon
  and the ark, 103
  historical context, 3, 11

Jeremiah on, 8
Jewish exiles, 108–9
John's depiction of, 109n18
siege, 45–52, 93, 105, 108–9
symbolic actions, 51–54
and Zedekiah, 13–15
Bar Cosiba, 68n7
Baruch, 11–13, 14
Ben-Gurion, David, 114
Book of Consolation
  arrangement, 101, 110
  concluding thoughts, 122–23
  general comments, 109–10
  leading themes, 110–16
  new covenant, 53, 118–22
  repentance and rebirth, 116–17
Book of Glory, 55–56
book of Psalms, 98
Book of Signs, 55–56
Book of the Law, 12–13
Bunyan, John, 98
buying a field, 53–55

call narrative, 3–8, 60
Canaan, 2, 5
Carchemish, 11, 43
categories of prophecies, 99–100
celibacy, 45–47
Cerinthus, 71
child sacrifice, 45–46n4
Christian America, 5n9, 33–37, 97–98, 104–5

135

Index

City of David, 48n6
civil religion, 35
cleansing of the temple, 57
Clinton, Hillary, 35–36
coincidences, 14n27
compassionate God, 108
complaints, 76–98
    fifth, 93–96
    first, 79–84
    fourth, 91–93
    introduction, 76–78
    overview of five, 78–79
    second, 84–88
    significance of, 97–98
    third, 88–91
consequences of covenant disloyalty, 46
conversion, 113
conviction, 74–75
Corinth, 73
counter symbolic actions, 50–52, 64–65, 70
covenants
    disobedience, 83
    lawsuit, 23–26
    new, 53, 101, 118–22
    temple sermon, 32–34
    violation, 118
cultic activity, 58n1

Damascus, 101
David
    and Bathsheba, 119n32
    divine promise, 121–22
    Psalm, 37, 81
    settlement of Canaan, 2
    and Solomon, 41, 113
David (City of), 10
Davidic dynasty, 24–25, 32, 105–6
David-Zion theology, 24–25
Day of Pentecost, 115
Deborah, 60
Deuteronomy, 15–16, 16n31, 63, 119

divine
    assurance of, 5, 14, 17–18
    forgiveness of, 107–8
    justice, 82–84
    oracle, 122
    promise, 114–15, 121–22
    protection of, 32
    response of, 90–91, 92–93, 96
Dome of the Rock, 104

Ebed-melech, 14, 59
Edom, 101
egalitarianism of prophets, 59–60
Egypt
    and Babylon, 3, 8, 11, 45, 51
    eschatological prophecies, 100–101
    exile in, 14–16
    and Jehoahaz, 20
eisegesis, 34
Eli, 2, 16, 26
Eliezer, 103
Elijah, 28, 46
Elisha, 28, 46
Elishama, 11
empirical tests, 63–65, 68–69
end times, 121–22
entrance liturgy, 21
environmental woes, 82
Ephraim, 26–27
eschatological prophecies, 99–123
ethical tests, 66, 72–74
Euphrates River, 42–44
Eusebius, 108
evangelical church, 35–38, 38n33
exile, 15
Ezekiel
    about, 17–18
    covenant, 101
    prophecies, 119–21
    symbolic actions, 40, 43, 101
Ezra, 52, 113

Index

false prophets, 58–75
  ethical test, 66, 72–74
  Holy Spirit, 74–75
  and the New Testament, 67–75
  second complaint, 84–85
  symbolic actions, 52
  tests for, 62–72
fifth complaint, 93–96
  setting, 93
  structure, 93–94
  substance, 94–96
fig tree, 30
first complaint, 79–84
  as familiar problem, 80–81
  flow of argument, 81–82
  God's answer, 82–84
  setting, 79–80
fourth complaint, 91–93
  setting, 91
  structure, 91
  substance, 92–93
futurity, 99–100

genuine prophets, 59–60, 62–63
Gnosticism, 70–72
God's love, 117
God's plan, 116–17
Gospel of John, 55–57, 74–75

Hanamel, 53–54
Hananiah
  counter symbolic actions, 50, 52–53, 63–66
Hannah, 16
Hasmonean dynasty, 113, 113n25
Hazor, 101
Hebrews, 121, 122
Hezekiah, 28
Hilkiah, 1, 1n2
Hinnom Valley, 49–50, 93
Holy Spirit, 74–75
Hophni, 2, 26
Hosea
  husband-wife imagery, 102

prophecies, 23–24
prophetic call narratives, 17
Huldah, 29n14, 60
husband-wife imagery, 102

incarnation, 70–72
individual responsibility, 119–20
Iron Age II, 10n22
Isaiah
  covenant lawsuit, 24
  moneychangers in the temple, 30
  regathering of exiles, 114
  righteous Branch, 106
  tasked as prophet, 4
  true prophet, 60
  visionary experience, 17–18
Israel
  as addressees of prophecies, 100
  and Christian America, 34
  dry season, 86–87n10
  exhorted not to fear, 107
  false prophets, 60
  fig tree, 30, 56
  God's love, 117
  and Jeremiah's vision of future, 100–105
  modern State of, 114
  new covenant, 53, 55, 118–22, 125–26
  Palestinian dispute, 115–16
  Pesach, 20
  prophetic call narratives, 7–8
  prophets/prophecy, 17–18
  regathering of exiles, 100
  restoration of, 101, 113
  return, 110, 115
  return to Zion, 102–5
  salvation of, 105–6
  symbolic actions, 48
  temple sermon, 23–28

Jacob, 100, 107
Jeconiah (Jecoiachin), 52, 103

Index

Jehoahaz, 19–20, 20n2
Jehoiakim
  bankrupt leadership, 103
  and Jeremiah, 10–13, 28–29
  and temple sermon, 19–22
Jehudi, 12
Jeremiah
  among the prophets, 16–18
  antisocial behavior, 45–46, 88–89
  ark of the covenant, 103–4
  birth and background, 1–2
  Book of Consolation, 109–10
  call and commission, 3–8
  celibacy, 45–47
  complaints, 76–98
  exhortation to Jacob passage, 107
  exile in Egypt, 15
  faithless Israel returns to Zion passage, 102–5
  false prophets, 58–75
  grief of, 83n6
  highlights of ministry, 8–15
  Holy Spirit, 74–75
  and Jehoiakim, 10–13, 28–29
  and Jesus, 10–13, 28–31
  and Josiah, 3, 9–10
  linen belt, 41–44
  meaning of name, 1–2
  and Moses, 15–16
  and Nebuchadnezzar, 51, 59
  new covenant, 118–22
  personal healing plea, 89–91
  pots and potsherds, 47–50, 93
  prophecies of return, 113
  remnant and righteous king passage, 105–6
  remnant returns and Yahweh removes their guilt passage, 107–8
  repentance, return, renewal passage, 107
  repentance and rebirth, 116–17
  scope of preaching, 100–101
  scroll read aloud, 12n24
  sermons, 6, ix–x
  settling the score and fleeing the premises passage, 108–9
  stocks episode, 93
  symbolic actions, 39–55, 93
  temple sermon, 19–38, 57
  tests for false prophets, 62–72
  treatment of, 89–91, 92–93, 95–96
  unjust accusations against, 91–93
  vilification of, 59
  vision of the future, 99–123
  visions, 48, 118–19
  vulnerability of, 85–87
  yoke action, 50–53, 63–65
  and Zedekiah, 8, 103
Jeroboam, 41
Jerusalem
  complaints, 91
  destruction of, 45–47, 53, 56
  destruction of temple, 5
  eschatological prophecies, 102, 105, 107–9
  false prophets, 60, 63–66
  historical context, 25
  and Jehoiakim, 10–11
  priesthood, 1–2, 17
  Sinai covenant, 8
  symbolic actions, 40–41, 43–50
  temple sermon, 28, 31
  and Zedekiah, 13–15
Jesse, 106
Jesus
  approach to enemies, 90
  celibacy, 47
  complaints, 88
  false prophets, 67–73
  following, 97–98
  on Holy Spirit, 74
  and Jeremiah, 10–13, 28–31
  and Judah, 113
  millennial reign, 112
  new covenant, 101

Index

New Testament, 106, 121–23
promise to apostles, 18
prophecy of return, 115–16
symbolic actions, 55–57
temple destruction, 5
and temple sermon, 19–22
Jewish exiles, 108, 110–15, 114n26, 116–17
Job
   complaints, 76–78, 81, 85, 95
John
   end-time Babylon, 109
   false prophets, 67, 70–75
   new covenant, 118, 121
   return to land, 112–13
   symbolic actions, 55–57
John the Baptist, 46–47, 72
Jonah, 60, 77–78, 87
   complaints, 77–78
Jordan Valley, 10
Joseph, 31
Josephus, 113
Joshua, 5
Josiah
   and the ark, 103–4
   ark of the covenant, 103–4
   false prophets, 58
   and Jehoiakim, 11–12
   and Jeremiah, 3, 9–10
   and Judah, 7–8
   temple sermon, 19–20
Judah
   as addressees of prophecies, 100
   and Babylon, 43, 64–65
   covenant disobedience, 83–84, 87
   false prophets, 60–61
   historical context, 3
   kings of, 8–10
   prophetic call narratives, 7–8
   return of exiles, 100
   return of land, 55
   Roman control of, 113–14
   salvation of, 105–6
   second complaint, 84
   temple sermon, 19–20, 24, 27, 32
   war against, 45–47
   and Zedekiah's reign, 51–52
Judaism, 70
Judaizers, 70
Judas Iscariot, 50
Judea. See Judah
judgment oracles, 6–7, 11, 23n6, 53, 61–62, 101, 122–23

Kedar, 101
Kiriath-jearim, 28

Lamentations, 13
Last Supper, 57, 121
linen belt, 41–45
   component parts, 42–44
   meaning of, 44–45
Luke, 4, 121

Maccabees, 104, 113
Manasseh, 45, 103
marginalized groups, 38n33
Mark, 56
Mary, 31
mass'a, 66–67
matrimony, 47
Matthew, 31, 50, 56
Megiddo, 8, 19
Melchizedek, 122
messianic Jews, 115–16
messianism, 68–69nn7–8, 106
Micah, 24, 28
Micaiah, 11
Mishnah, 103–4
Moab, 10, 100–101
Molech, 50
moral test, 66
Moresheth, 28
Mosaic covenant, 16
Moses
   complaints, 76, 84, 88, 92
   divine assurance, 5
   and Jeremiah, 15–16

Index

Moses *(continued)*
  and prophecy, 55, 60
  reluctance to serve, 4
  Ten Commandments, 20
mourning, denial of, 45–47
Mt. Nebo, 16, 104
Mt. Sinai, 100, 120

Nahman, 103–4
narrative, 53
Nathan, 24, 28
national ideology, 32
national restoration, 101
Nebuchadnezzar, 59
  ark of the covenant, 103
  Babylonian invasion, 80
  and Hananiah's counter symbolic action, 63–64
  and Jehoiakim, 11
  and Jeremiah, 51, 59
  and war against Judah, 8, 45
  and Zedekiah, 14, 122
Neco II, 8, 19, 20n2
Nehemiah, 113
Neo-Babylonian, 7, 11
new covenant, 118–22
  ark, 104
  and false prophets, 67–75
  spiritual struggles, 97–98
  symbolic acts in, 55–57
  women prophets in, 60
New Testament
  Babylonian siege, 50
  and Christian America, 34, 84
  messianic text, 106
  new covenant, 33, 121–22, 126
  and Old Testament, 112
  Paul in, 4, 17
  redemption, 55
  symbolic actions, 55–57
Noadiah, 60
Noah, 118
Nob, 2
Nubia, 14n26

Old Testament
  ark of the covenant, 103
  false prophets, 60, 68
  proclamation, 99–100n2
  prophecy, 99n2
  regathering and return, 112
  symbolic actions, 52–53, 57
  Yahweh's preordination, 3–4
Ophel ridge, 10, 12
oracles, 60–61
"Oracles against the Nation," 100–101

Pashhur, 93–95
Paul
  as apostle, 17–18
  call narrative, 4
  celibacy, 47
  false prophets, 67, 70, 72–73
  Jewish peoples, 112–13
  on mystery, 116
  new covenant, 121
  reflection as in a mirro, 125
  symbolic actions, 56
Perath, 42–44
persecution, 4
Pesach, 20
Peter
  and evangelism, 37
  false prophets, 67, 69, 72–73
  on fear, 18
  prophecies of return, 115
Philistia, 100–101
Phinehas, 2, 26
pilgrimage festivals, 20
Pilgrim and Puritan theology, 33–34
planned symbolic actions, 40–41
poetic oracles, 109–10
pots and potsherds, 47–50, 93
Potsherd Gate, 93
praying for destruction of enemies, 90n11
premeditated symbolic action, 40–41

Index

premillennialism, 111–12
preordination, 3–4
priests/priesthood, 1n1, 2
proclamation, 6, 99n2
prophet/prophecy
  Book of Consolation, 101–6
  call narratives, 3–7, 16–17
  Davidic king, 105–6
  and Eli, 2
  eschatological, 99–101
  fulfillment of, 122
  Jeremiah, 13–17
  judgment oracles, 23–24
  literature, 42–43
  qualifications of, 59–60
  of return, 115
  and symbolic actions, 39–41, 52
  temple sermon, 28–29
  tests for, 62–72
prose narrative and oracles, 110
prosperity gospel, 97n16
protest, 4–5
Protestant theological divide, 111–12
providence, 35
Psalm 37, 81
Psalm 73, 81
Psalter, 21n3
Psammeticus II, 51
public markets, 30n17

racism, 38
Ramat Raḥel, 10, 12
real actions, 42–43
realpolitik, 10
rebirth, 116–17
reconciliation, 115–16
redemption, 55
redemptive history, 101
reformation, 46, 48
Reformed theology, 111–12
regathering of exiles, 110–14, 120
remnant, 105–6, 108–15, 117
repentance, 21, 27, 46, 48, 88, 107–8, 116–17

restoration
  of Israel, 101, 118
  oracles, 110
  poems, 118
resurrection of Jesus, 56
return to the land, 105–6, 110–15
righteous Branch, 106
royal dynasties, 59n3

salvation oracle, 102–6
Samaria, 61
Samuel
  call narrative, 4
  complaints, 92
  and Eli, 16
  symbolic actions, 40
Saul, 2, 40
Scriptures, 3, 12, 34, 104
scroll, 11–12
second complaint, 84–88
  setting, 84–85
  speech of Yahweh, 88
  structure, 85
  substance of, 85–87
Second Temple, 29–31, 52
Sennacherib, 25
Sermon on the Mount, 73
sermons, ix–x
Shaphan, 28–29
shepherds, civil leaders as, 102–3
Shiloh, 2, 26, 26n12
sign-acts. See symbolic actions
Simeon, 31
Sinai, 32
  covenant, 8–9, 20, 23, 25, 55, 58, 66–67, 118
  narratives, 16
Slough of Despond, 98
sola Scriptura (Scripture alone), 34
Solomon
  and Abiathar, 2
  and Ahijah, 41
  covenant disobedience, 25
  and Hasmonean dynasty, 113

Index

sovereignty vs. contingency, 48
spiritual desolation, 78n1
spiritualization of exile, 112–13
spiritual struggles, 97–98
spontaneous symbolic actions, 40
State of Israel, 114
submission to authority, 51–52
Succoth, 20
Sumer, 7
symbolic actions
   buying a field, 53–55
   celibacy of Jeremiah, 45–47
   cleansing of the temple, 57
   counter actions, 50–52, 64–65x, 70
   fig tree, 30, 56
   and Hananiah, 52–53, 63–66
   Last Supper, 57
   linen belt, 41–44
   in the New Testament, 55–57
   pots and potsherds, 47–50, 93
   premeditated, 40–41
   and prophecy, 39–41, 52
   resurrection of Jesus, 56
   spontaneous, 40
   yoke action, 50–53, 63–65
syncretism, 35
Synoptic Gospels, 56–57

Tahpanhes, 15
Temple Institute, 122n35
Temple Mount, 12
temple sermon, 11, 19–32, 57
Ten Commandments, 20, 23, 119
Tertullian, 15
theodicy, 80–81
theological tests, 63–65, 70–72
third complaint, 88–91
   setting, 88–89
   structure, 89
   substance, 89–91
third temple, 104–5
Topheth, 45, 50, 93
true prophets. See also prophet/prophecy

qualifications, 59–60
tests for, 62–72
Trump, Donald, 36–38

Uriah, 28

Valley of Slaughter, 50
vengeance, 95–96, 108
visionary actions, 42–43, 48
visions, 6–7, 6n14, 17–18

Washington, George, 32
witness for Christ, 17
women as prophets, 60

Yahweh
   complaints, 76–98
   divine promise of regathering, 114–15
   eschatological prophecies, 100, 102–9
   false prophets, 58–67
   and Jeremiah, 3–8, 11–13
   and Moses, 15–16
   name, 1–2n3
   new covenant, 118–20
   symbolic actions, 39–56
   temple sermon, 20, 22–29, 32
   and Zedekiah, 13–14
Yohai, 103

Zechariah, 106
Zedekiah
   about, 13–15
   complaints, 96
   and Jeremiah's ministry, 8
   and Jeremiah's vision of future, 103
   latter part of reign, 105–6
   new covenant, 121–22
   symbolic actions, 51–52
Zion, 24–25, 107
Zionism, 114
Zion theology, 32

www.ingramcontent.com/pod-product-compliance
Lightning Source LLC
Chambersburg PA
CBHW031434150426
43191CB00006B/518